PENGUIN BOOKS

YOU WANT ME TO WORK WITH WHO?

JULIE JANSEN has made five career changes within broadcasting, contingency recruiting, outplacement, and training industries in order to find work that fulfills and satisfies her professional and personal needs. She is a career coach, a consultant, and the author of *I Don't Know What I Want, but I Know It's Not This,* and helps both individuals and companies to be successful in the workplace. Jansen has been featured in publications such as *Psychology Today, Fortune, Cosmopolitan, Woman's Day, Essence,* and *Fitness,* and on CareerBuilder.com, and is a regular guest on national TV and radio. A frequent speaker at associations, corporations, and non-profit groups throughout the United States, she lives in Greenwich, Connecticut.

For more information, visit the author's Web site at www .juliejansen.net.

Also by Julie Jansen

I Don't Know What I Want, but I Know It's Not This:
A Step-by-Step Guide to Finding Gratifying Work

You Want Me to Work with Who?

Eleven Keys to a
Stress-Free,
Satisfying, and Successful
Work Life . . .
No Matter Who
You Work With

Julie Jansen

PENGUIN BOOKS

PENGUIN BOOKS

Published by the Penguin Group

Penguin Group (USA) Inc., 375 Hudson Street, New York, New York 10014, U.S.A.
Penguin Group (Canada), 90 Eglinton Avenue East, Suite 700, Toronto, Ontario,
Canada M4P 2Y3 (a division of Pearson Penguin Canada Inc.)
Penguin Books Ltd, 80 Strand, London WC2R 0RL, England
Penguin Ireland, 25 St Stephen's Green, Dublin 2, Ireland
(a division of Penguin Books Ltd)
Penguin Group (Australia), 250 Camberwell Road, Camberwell, Victoria 3124,
Australia (a division of Pearson Australia Group Pty Ltd)
Penguin Books India Pvt Ltd, 11 Community Centre,
Panchsheel Park, New Delhi - 110 017, India
Penguin Group (NZ), cnr Airborne and Rosedale Roads,
Albany, Auckland 1310, New Zealand
(a division of Pearson New Zealand Ltd)
Penguin Books (South Africa) (Pty) Ltd, 24 Sturdee Avenue,
Rosebank, Johannesburg 2196, South Africa

Penguin Books Ltd, Registered Offices:
80 Strand, London WC2R 0RL, England

First published in Penguin Books 2006

3   5   7   9   10   8   6   4   2

LIBRARY OF CONGRESS CATALOGING-IN-PUBLICATION DATA
Jansen, Julie.
You want me to work with who? : eleven keys to a stress-free, satisfying, and successful
work life—no matter who you work with / Julie Jansen.
p. cm.
Includes index.
ISBN 0 14 30.3680 7
1. Office politics.   2. Emotional intelligence.   3. Interpersonal relations.
4. Conflict management.   5. Success in business.   I. Title.
HF5386.5.J36 2006
650.1'3—dc22   2005053911

Printed in the United States of America
Set in Berkeley
Designed by BTD NYC

This book is dedicated to Deb Ziegler.
I miss you.

Acknowledgments

As every author knows, it is impossible to write a book without the ideas, advice, and support of other people. I am a fortunate person to have so many wonderful relationships, and I wish I could fill this book with thanks to everyone in my life. This said, I'd like to express my heartfelt gratitude to all my friends and colleagues who believe in me, encourage me, and especially who respected my need to disappear while I was writing this book.

Big thanks to my agent, Denise Marcil, who is unfailingly supportive and really talented at what she does. Jane von Mehren, you fought for me and my idea as you always have. Brett Kelly, you're a treasure as an editor and a person. How lucky am I?

To all my clients whom I can't name here for confidentiality reasons. Thank you for believing in me. You know who you are.

Lora Friedman, your creativity, voice of reason, and editing skills made this book. Devin Comiskey, my research guru . . . thank you for helping me shortcut the process a hundredfold. Bonnie Depp, you are amazing in a crunch, and your vision and common sense made the revision process bearable.

Ben, my S.O. and honey. No one in my life is more supportive and more of a fan than you are. I love you. Momster, I can see where Ben gets his loving nature. You are always there for me.

Popsie, your pride in me is touching and means the world to me. Melody, who said stepmothers are wicked? I've always known how lucky I am to be part of you.

Chris, my brother. Your resourcefulness and willingness to help me when I've been stuck while I was writing this book have saved me so many times.

My sister Kim, whose job experiences gave me good material to work with.

Chris Beggs, you're so much to me in so many ways. I couldn't imagine life without you, my dear friend.

Robert Montello, you are a kind and generous soul.

Diana "Disie" Carter, no one makes me smile or laugh the way you do. And John, I adore you, too.

Last, my two "girls," Sophie and Violet. The best company an author could ask for. Meow!

Contents

Introduction

WHY CAN'T WE ALL JUST GET ALONG?

"I'd really like my job if only I didn't have to work with other people!" This simple statement may sound laughable at first, but it actually reflects a serious problem in the workplace that has reached epidemic proportions.

One of the biggest causes of stress in the work environment is the inability of colleagues, at all levels, to get along with one another. While knowledge, experience, education, and skills certainly contribute to any individual's success at work, it's the quality of an employee's relationships with bosses, coworkers, and clients that will ultimately determine his or her happiness and productivity in the workplace. In other words, if you have difficulty relating to or coexisting with other people at work, your chances of having a satisfying and successful work life will be severely limited.

The first time that most people *really* realize this is when they run into a thorny problem, conflict, or misunderstanding with someone at work. The incident soon becomes a situation, and the situation takes on a life of its own. It either keeps recurring or remains unresolved until a major upheaval or unwanted change becomes inevitable.

Why is it so hard to work with other people? There are many reasons.

Reason #1: People Are Difficult

Difficult people are everywhere, and each one exhibits a different brand of bad behavior. In other words, anyone who behaves in a way that irritates you or who does something that you don't want them to do can be labeled a difficult person.

When Manchester Consulting, a national outplacement firm, surveyed 358 U.S. organizations about the most serious behavioral problems among their senior management, "poor communication skills" was ranked number one. "Poor interpersonal skills" was cited as the major employee-relations problem of top-level executives.

Regardless of what the specific traits are, there are many difficult people in the workplace, and there always will be.

Reason #2: Work Is Stressful

Constant change, competition, technology, globalization, sterile work environments, unrealistic expectations, and the endless pressure to communicate instantly, without much thought or reflection—all typical of today's workplace—can create an environment so stressful that it can bring out the worst in any person, even one who is typically pleasant and easygoing.

Reason #3: Employers Don't Facilitate People Problems

Many companies talk up the importance of working as a team, collaborating and creating consensus, yet offer compensation plans and reward systems geared solely toward individual contribution and achievement. Sound familiar? This mixed message, prevalent in many companies today, can promote competition and insecurity, which can lead to self-centered, self-preserving behavior on the part of employees, which always results in strained working relationships. Unfortunately many companies don't anticipate these issues and don't do much to handle them once they have occurred. The general consensus is that everyone is too busy to deal with people problems, focusing instead on business results.

Reason #4: People Have Problems

Personal issues can prevent anyone from nurturing and sustaining healthy relationships at work. If you're bored, stressed out from overwork or family problems or generally frustrated or depressed, you are at high risk for neglecting or abusing your relationships with colleagues or clients. Unhappiness breeds unhappiness. Walking around with your head in a dark cloud can lead to friction or misunderstandings between you and the people with whom you spend at least half your waking hours—your coworkers.

Reason #5: People Are Complex

Most companies try to hire employees who will fit into their specific corporate culture. Even if employers are reasonably successful at making the "right hires," each individual they bring on board still has personal baggage—expectations, biases, memories, perceptions, family dynamics, values, ways of doing things, and intangible qualities—that he carries with him onto the ship. This unpredictable mix of different personalities, communication styles, and work habits can lead to confusion, miscommunication, and conflict.

WHAT CAN YOU DO ABOUT IT?

If you work with other people, it's inevitable that at some point you will be party to a serious miscommunication, get involved in a conflict or disagreement, or simply fail to connect on a personal level with a boss or coworker. In addition to skills, knowledge, and experience, there are Eleven Keys to getting along with anyone. Some people don't possess many of them, others possess most of them but are missing a few crucial ones, but all Eleven Keys are essential to dealing positively with other people's flaws and deficiencies.

You will learn much more about the Eleven Keys throughout this book. They are arranged alphabetically, not in the order that they may fall organically. Here's a quick rundown. They are:

Key #1—CONFIDENCE
Key #2—CURIOSITY
Key #3—DECISIVENESS
Key #4—EMPATHY

Key #5—FLEXIBILITY
Key #6—HUMOR
Key #7—INTELLIGENCE
Key #8—OPTIMISM
Key #9—PERSEVERANCE
Key #10—RESPECT
Key #11—SELF-AWARENESS

There is no question that learning techniques for dealing with difficult people can be useful, and the Keys will help you do this. But working harmoniously and productively with people on a day-to-day basis is much more involved than simply knowing how to handle a bully, a know-it-all, or a complainer. Like it or not, you will need to get in touch with yourself and really understand which of your characteristics are effective and which you really could improve. Your ability to develop or strengthen specific Keys, or tone them down, will determine how well you are able to cope with different situations and succeed at influencing, persuading, relating to, understanding, connecting with, or collaborating with others.

The theme you'll hear repeatedly in this book is that *it's up to you to get along with others!* Much as we wish that people would change, if they don't have a meaningful incentive or motive for working well with others, they won't. The main message of this book is that you, the reader, can be in control of your situation at work by using the Eleven Keys to strengthen yourself and manage your relationships, especially the challenging ones.

The Eleven Keys can open the door to success not only in your work life but also in your personal life. As you read through the book, you'll quickly decide which of the Eleven Keys have the most meaning for you. You'll be able to identify which ones those difficult people in your work life possess, which ones they may need more of, and which they may need to tone down. You'll then be able to go through the same process for yourself. Practical, step-by-step self-assessment tools, an annotated resource guide, and personal stories from people who have faced all kinds of challenging experiences at work and have handled them with varying degrees of success (based upon their ability to use one or more of the Eleven Keys) will help you derive the maximum benefit from this guide. What's vital is your ability to adapt and to be open to approaching your coworkers in a different way so that while they may not always get along with each other, they'll always get along with you.

You Want Me to Work with Who?

Part I

THE ELEVEN KEYS
and
DIFFICULT PEOPLE

The Eleven Keys

Since Daniel Goleman coined the term "emotional intelligence" in 1995 with his best-selling book of the same name, we've heard a lot about this concept, and how while successful leaders usually exhibit traits such as toughness, intelligence, determination, and vision, they are also distinguished by what are commonly categorized as "softer" skills, such as self-awareness, self-regulation, motivation, and empathy.

The Eleven Keys, which are the central focus of this book, are based on this principle of emotional intelligence, but combine a few additional "harder" traits. They are drawn from my twenty years of interacting with all kinds of people in the workplace. Time and again, I have observed that individuals who have the Eleven Keys and *know how to use them in a balanced way* tend to be more successful and well-liked by their colleagues than people who don't possess them. They also experience less stress than others because, by properly utilizing the Eleven Keys, they are better equipped to handle people who have difficult personality traits and to gain control of their work relationships, and are more likely to build up a functioning immunity to problematic people. While it is impossible to change other people's inherent personality traits, it is absolutely within the realm of possibility to be in control of our relationships with difficult people and to find peace and balance. This is what the Eleven Keys will do for you.

THE ELEVEN KEYS ARE:

1. **Confidence**—The capacity to believe in yourself and your choices; to take pleasure in your relationships and pride in your accomplishments; and to view yourself and your situation realistically.

2. **Curiosity**—An eagerness to understand, to know, and to learn; intense and sincere interest in investigating and exploring the unknown.

3. **Decisiveness**—The ability to make choices based on a combination of analysis, critical thinking, and judgment; arriving at conclusions and making decisions with determination and confidence, even in the absence of adequate time or information.

4. **Empathy**—The capacity to demonstrate caring and understanding of someone else's situation, feelings, and motives; to imagine what it might be like to walk in someone else's shoes, especially when you've never worn them.

5. **Flexibility**—Being capable of and responding positively to change, both internal and external; being pliable, adaptable, nonrigid, and able to deal well with ambiguity.

6. **Humor**—The ability to view oneself and the world with enjoyment; a talent for not taking life, or oneself, too seriously; being amusing, amused, and, at times, even comical.

7. **Intelligence**—The ability to work cleverly, creatively, and efficiently; to plan before taking action; to use critical thinking, logic, and analysis to solve problems, form opinions, and arrive at conclusions. Managing time effectively, taking creative approaches, and communicating clearly and effectively.

8. **Optimism**—Expecting the best possible outcome and dwelling on the most hopeful or positive aspects of a situation, even in the face of adversity.

9. **Perseverance**—The passion, energy, focus, and desire to get results; being unwilling to quit until the job gets done. Motivation, persistence, and hard work, as well as consistent follow-through, "closing the loop," and taking the next step to move the process forward.

10. **Respect**—Treating others in a considerate, gracious, and thoughtful manner; protecting another person's self-esteem; being profes-

sional in your communication; following through on promises and commitments; behaving with integrity; remembering that it's just as easy to be nice as it is to be nasty; not using mean behavior to instill fear or maintain control over others.

11. **Self-awareness**—The ability to recognize, understand, and manage your own moods, emotions, and drives, as well as to understand their effect on others.

Now that you've learned about the Eleven Keys, think about someone you work with who causes you stress. Which of the Eleven Keys would you count among his or her strengths? Which ones might he or she lack? Or tend to overuse?

Now, do the same exercise with yourself. If you are not sure (perhaps because your Self-awareness is weak), ask several people whom you trust which of the Eleven Keys, in their opinion, are your strengths and which you may need to work on. While few people possess all Eleven Keys in equal amounts, virtually anyone can develop and master the use of any of the Keys. Take a few moments to review the Eleven Keys. Then, take this self-assessment exercise to further identify which Keys you need to develop, tone down, or balance, particularly at work.

The questions are grouped by the Eleven Keys. Read each one carefully, then select the answer that **most closely** describes the way you would react or behave. For best results, answer as quickly and easily as you can, without laboring over your response.

Confidence

1. You're late to a staff meeting and your boss stops talking when you walk in the room and comments about your tardiness. You:
    a. Coolly remark that his observation skills are as sharp as ever.
    b. Say that you're sorry and explain why you were late.
    c. Apologize to everyone in the room and tell your boss you'll be happy to do whatever is needed to learn what you missed.

2. Your coworker compliments you on what you're wearing. You say:
    a. "Yes, I look pretty good in this, don't I?"
    b. "Thank you very much, it's one of my favorite outfits!"
    c. "This? It was on sale and it would look a lot better if I could lose ten pounds."

3. Your boss asks you to take on a project in a high-visibility area you know very little about. You:
    a. Agree immediately and tell her it's about time you've been given a plum assignment like this one.
    b. Thank her and ask her what resources will be available for you to use so that you will be successful.
    c. Tell her that you need to think about it and stay awake all night worrying about what you should do.

4. You worked very hard on a presentation for an important client and afterward got feedback from the client that he was disappointed. You:
    a. E-mail him and tell him that you put a lot of effort into the presentation and you can't understand why he was dissatisfied.
    b. Call him and ask him how soon you can get together to discuss what was missing and what to do next.
    c. Send him an e-mail apologizing for disappointing him.

5. One of your direct reports approaches you and tells you that she feels as if you undermine her in meetings. You:
    a. Feel surprised and deny that you do this to her.
    b. Thank her for having the courage to tell you and suggest that you sit down together to discuss it.
    c. Apologize profusely and tell her that you'll never do it again.

Curiosity

1. Your work is the most fulfilling and enjoyable when you:
    a. Are constantly learning new things every day.

    b. Have a balance of both predictable and new tasks and projects.

    c. Know exactly what to expect every day.

2. When was the last time you had a completely new or unique experience?
   a. Just recently.
   b. In the last year.
   c. I honestly can't remember.

3. Your manager asks you to come up with a new approach for a business problem. You:
   a. Excitedly plan to read as much as you can, interview people, benchmark best practices, and study everything you can get your hands on before getting started.
   b. Do a little interviewing of people who have dealt with the same type of problem and then write a brief plan.
   c. Get started right away—you've wanted to sink your teeth into the situation for a long time.

4. Your colleagues would describe you as:
   a. Someone who is constantly seeking out new ways of doing things even when change isn't necessary.
   b. Someone who is interested in other people and new ideas.
   c. Someone who is steady and content with the way things are.

5. Which one of the following statements best describes you?
   a. I need to search for answers, speculate about things, and experience new sensations as much as possible.
   b. I fill my spare time with interesting activities and love learning new things whenever I can.
   c. If something interests me, I pursue it; otherwise, I'm not that inquisitive.

Decisiveness

Choose the answer you agree with most.

1. When you have a problem to solve at work, most of the time you make up your mind immediately about how you will solve it.
    a. Yes, 90 percent of the time I take action right away.
    b. It depends on the resources and people I need to solve the problem.
    c. Not usually, because I need to think things through for a while.

2. You have decided to look for a new job but are unsure about what type of job to pursue because you are tired of your industry. You:
    a. Update your résumé and start answering ads on Monster.com.
    b. Identify a decision-making process first before doing anything.
    c. Don't do anything because you aren't sure what approach to take.

3. The last time you made a decision about something major like moving, changing jobs, or breaking up with someone, you:
    a. Took action right after you made the decision to make a change.
    b. Balanced your gut reaction with some analysis first before deciding what to do.
    c. Vacillated a lot and ended up making a decision when you felt pressed up against the wall.

4. When making decisions, other people's opinions are:
    a. Not that important to me.
    b. Meaningful if the decisions involve other people. Otherwise, I trust my own gut.
    c. Important input for most of my decisions.

5. Is making the right decision every time important to you?
    a. There are many ways to approach a situation. Making a quick decision is the most important thing.
    b. Not necessarily, as long as I've been thoughtful about making my decision.
    c. Absolutely! Otherwise people won't trust me.

Empathy

Choose the answer you agree with most.

1. When you are in a meeting with a senior executive at your company or a client, the most important thing is to understand their emotions and motives.
    a. Yes, because I want my hallmark at work to be that I truly feel what others are feeling.
    b. Yes, sure, but I honestly think preparation and achieving business objectives are just as important.
    c. Not really. I don't think emotion has a place in business.

2. Your job doesn't give you a huge opportunity to help others so you do some volunteer work for organizations you believe in.
    a. Yes, I probably care more about the work I do as a volunteer than I do about my job.
    b. Yes, this is true, and I really get fulfillment and meaning from my volunteering.
    c. No, unfortunately I either don't have the time or interest in volunteering.

3. You manage people in your job and find it a bit difficult to relate to some of your direct reports' problems at times.
    a. Never. My favorite part of my job is managing people and helping them deal with life's problems, both professionally and personally.
    b. Sometimes, but I do try to understand my staff so that I can be as compassionate as possible.
    c. Yes, this is definitely true! I find myself losing patience quite often with my staff and all their personal problems.

4. You are appropriately sympathetic to other people when necessary; however, you really like to stick to business if you can.
    a. No way. People are human and I think that just sticking to business is a little cold.

b. I am well aware of my job and the accomplishments I need to achieve; however, I prefer a very balanced approach to interacting with others at work.

c. Yes, I agree with this statement. If I focus on business only, it makes it easier to get things done.

5. You are interviewing a candidate for an open position that reports to you. You:

a. Focus your questions on the person's motives and emotional and psychological state.

b. Balance your questions between behavioral, skill-related, and the candidate's motives.

c. Ask the candidate questions mostly about his work history.

Flexibility

Choose the answer you agree with most.

1. You have a proposal to write, your biweekly report is due tomorrow, and you need to reply to at least thirty-five e-mails. Your boss pops his head into your office and asks you to stand in for him and give a quick speech at a lunch meeting today. You:

a. Say, "Sure, no problem," sighing inwardly because you know it's going to be another day of burning the midnight oil.

b. Smile at him and jokingly say, "Hope my annual increase is *really* big this year." When he leaves, you decide to stop and reprioritize your projects.

c. Scowl, then say, "Do you have any idea of the deadlines I have this week? Can't you get Josh to do it?"

2. Your client sends you an e-mail asking if you can send her all the documentation you have on the project you're working on with her. She doesn't tell you why she wants the information. You:

a. Respond that you'll get everything to her by noon tomorrow even though you know you'll have to drop everything to get it done.

      b. Send her an e-mail asking if you can schedule a phone call or, better, a meeting to understand exactly what she needs.

      c. E-mail her telling her that you're really busy this week and that you'll try to get to it by next week.

3. You're self-employed and business is slow. One of your few clients calls you asking you to do some work immediately with no lead time and at a low fee. You:

      a. Say you'll do it right away without trying to negotiate anything.

      b. Tell him how thrilled you are that he thought of you for this project, and ask him if you can spend some time discussing the project scope, budget, and his expectations.

      c. Tell him that you couldn't possibly do work this immediately and at that kind of fee!

4. It is halfway through your company's fiscal year and the department you work in isn't hitting its numbers. Your manager asks you and your coworkers to re-assess the way you're doing your jobs to measure productivity and profitability. You:

      a. Respond, "Anything you need me to do boss!"

      b. Tell your manager that you'd like to be a partner with him in helping him rationalize the department's viability.

      c. Skulk out of his office, vowing not to cooperate in this plot to ruin your department.

5. Your coworker tends to rely on you a little too much to help him with his weekly reports. He happens to be your boss's nephew. You:

      a. Never say no to helping him.

      b. Help him only when you can take the time from your work.

      c. Tell him that you think he leans on you to finish his work because of his relationship with your manager and that you refuse to help him ever again!

Humor

Choose the answer you agree with most.

1. True or false: There isn't a situation at work that couldn't use a little humor.
   a. True by all means! Humor is absolutely a must in every situation!
   b. Not necessarily, it depends on the situation and who is involved.
   c. False, humor does not have a place at work.

2. You tend to take your work and yourself a little too seriously at times.
   a. No way! I joke and laugh as much as I can at work.
   b. I really balance using humor and being serious well.
   c. Yes, this is the feedback I've gotten from people.

3. The last time you laughed out loud at work was:
   a. Within the last day.
   b. Within a few weeks.
   c. I can't remember.

4. When you are dealing with someone at work with a difficult personality, you remember to use humor as a technique for getting along with him or her.
   a. Are you kidding? I joke all the time no matter whom I'm interacting with.
   b. Yes, I do realize that this can work and try to do it whenever possible.
   c. No, because I think that most difficult people are too self-absorbed to have a sense of humor.

5. When something goes wrong at work, you immediately try to see the humor in it instead of dwelling on the negative aspects.
   a. Yes, it's my favorite technique for dealing with a tough situation!
   b. Sometimes this works, sometimes it doesn't.
   c. I find it hard to see the humor in a situation that goes wrong right away because I'm usually too stressed.

Intelligence

Choose the answer you agree with most.

1. When you undertake a new responsibility in your job, you:
   a. Stop and analyze what you already know and what you have to learn, and then start doing whatever it is you have to.
   b. Try to find someone else who has done it before, and talk to him first before doing anything.
   c. Put your head down and just start doing whatever it is you need to get done.

2. When you make a mistake, you:
   a. Sit and spend a lot of time thinking about why you made the mistake and what you'd do differently in the future.
   b. Shrug and reassure yourself that everyone makes mistakes.
   c. Get annoyed with yourself and focus on the mistake rather than on what you could have done differently.

3. You are working on something that involves a large amount of detail. When you've finished, you:
   a. Ask someone else in your department to read it carefully.
   b. Sit down and read through it very slowly and carefully.
   c. Give it to your boss after skimming it quickly because you've done it so many times before.

4. You notice that some numbers don't make sense in a report that you compile regularly using data other people provide. You:
   a. Call or e-mail the people who give you information for the report, asking them to recheck their numbers and resend them.
   b. Read through the report again to check if you made a mistake.
   c. Make assumptions about why the numbers are off and send out the report the way it is.

5. You've tried to do something technical several times without success. You:

    a. Go to the person who explained it to you and ask for it to be explained in a different way.

    b. Keep trying with the hope that you'll figure it out eventually.

    c. Throw your hands in the air and stop trying.

Optimism

Choose the answer you agree with most.

1. It's been a bad day—you had a flat tire, you were an hour late for an important meeting, and your child was sent home from school sick. You:

    a. Think to yourself that this is all part of life and you're grateful to be healthy.

    b. Call your best friend and joke about "bad luck coming in threes."

    c. Get depressed and wonder what bad thing is going to happen next.

2. You get laid off from your job. You:

    a. Feel very excited about finding a new job or even changing careers despite media reports of high unemployment.

    b. Sit and think about the opportunities and obstacles that exist in your situation.

    c. Immediately call the bank to apply for a loan to refinance your mortgage.

3. Life has been pretty tough for a while now. Your marriage isn't great, you and your boss aren't getting along, and you've incurred several large unexpected expenses. You:

    a. Tell yourself that you have no right to feel sorry for yourself because you and your loved ones are all healthy.

    b. Remind yourself that things will get better and that you are the only one who can improve them.

    c. Feel that you're the cause of all your troubles and that things are never going to improve.

4. You gave a speech at your company's sales meeting and afterward your boss pulled you aside and suggested that you hire a presentation-skills coach. You:
   a. Nod and tell him that you intend to become the best professional speaker he has ever heard in his life.
   b. Thank him for his suggestion and go right back to your office and begin researching presentation-skills coaches.
   c. Feeling very embarrassed, tell him that you were never good at public speaking and that you never will be.

5. You believe that someone who is lucky:
   a. Is someone who creates it for himself.
   b. Possesses a combination of right time, right place, and effort and skill.
   c. Someone who is born with it.

Perseverance

Choose the answer you agree with most.

1. One of your colleagues was just promoted into a position you think you should have been considered for. You:
   a. Decide to launch an all-out campaign to let everyone know that you want to be seriously considered as a candidate for the next similar position that becomes available.
   b. Discreetly begin to network with some of the key players in your organization to learn how to get noticed.
   c. Retreat into your office or cube and feel sorry for yourself.

2. You think that setting goals is important to do; however, when the goal is too difficult, you tend to get discouraged and give up.
   a. Never! I very rarely stop persisting until I achieve my goals.
   b. I usually try hard to accomplish a goal, but I need to have the right support and resources in order to do so.
   c. I'm not very goal oriented.

3. You believe that motivation is a combination of external and internal forces.
   a. It's great to have a healthy support system and environment, but deep down I know that motivation comes mostly from inside me.
   b. It's a constant balance to keep motivated consistently, especially when times are tough, but I do try.
   c. Actually, I am not very motivated if I don't get constant recognition and support from my boss and my family.

4. People who know me describe me as passionate, focused, and hardworking.
   a. Absolutely!
   b. Yes, if I'm interested in something.
   c. Probably not.

5. True or false: If someone is motivated and persistent about reaching his goals, he was born this way.
   a. False. Anyone can learn these things.
   b. It depends. These qualities are somewhat related to personality, which people are born with.
   c. True, and if they aren't born with these traits, it's very difficult to acquire them.

Respect

Choose the answer you agree with most.

1. Professionalism and sensitivity seem to be disappearing in the workplace.
   a. Yes, I've noticed this, and I pride myself on having impeccable manners and displaying courtesy to others at all times.
   b. Probably, and I know I'm a little guilty of being rushed and abrupt with others at times.
   c. I think it varies from person to person.

2. You are often reluctant to express an opinion in meetings unless it's positive.
   a. Of course not. I don't care if I am controversial as long as I'm heard.

    b. It really depends on the issue or topic being discussed and who's in the
       meeting.

    c. Yes, this is true. I am more concerned about hurting other people's
       feelings and being professional than about contributing my ideas.

3. You have sworn at work, yelled at someone, or asked someone to do something
   without saying please or thank you more than twice in the last month.
    a. Never!
    b. Well, maybe, but it's not usual behavior for me.
    c. Yes, even more than twice.

4. Once in a while you are guilty of taking the last cup of coffee or not filling the
   copier with paper—you've even "borrowed" someone's soda or yogurt from the
   refrigerator.
    a. Absolutely not.
    b. Yes, on rare occasions I've done these things.
    c. Oops, more often than I want to admit!

Self-awareness

Choose the answer you agree with most.

1. During a recent performance review with your boss, you found yourself quite
   surprised by his feedback about your attitude or behavior.
    a. No, I can honestly say that this hasn't ever happened to me.
    b. Maybe a little bit, but once I had time to think about what he said, I
       realized his feedback was on target.
    c. Yes, this actually did happen to me, and it wasn't the first time in my
       career either!

2. You always stop and think about how the things you say and do will affect others before you move ahead.
    a. Yes, nearly 100 percent of the time. It's so important to me to be
       completely in tune with myself and how I impact others.

b. Yes, but only when I am going to make an important presentation or face another significant event.

c. No, I can't say that I really ever stop to think about the implications of my actions and words.

3. You believe that you can change your attitude and behavior very easily to suit any situation.

a. Oh, without a question! I am always able to shift my attitude and behavior because I am aware of myself in every situation.

b. It really depends on the situation.

c. No, I am who I am, and at this point in life, I really don't think I can change.

4. When someone you know tells you that you're not listening or are behaving badly, you are sometimes taken aback by their comments.

a. Yes, I do take this kind of feedback seriously, especially because I already am aware that I am behaving this way, and the reinforcement is helpful.

b. It really depends on who is giving me the feedback. I think I know whether or not their feedback is accurate.

c. This is usually true. I am often surprised by other's perception of me.

5. Think back to a situation at work you were involved in that was contentious. Did you lose control of your emotions?

a. Actually, I haven't ever lost control in stressful situations with other people. I'm too aware of what the negative impact would be.

b. Yes, I have on occasion but managed to gain control.

c. Unfortunately, I am always emotional when I get into a conflict or have to deal with a difficult person.

SCORE KEY

Beginning with Confidence, write the total times you answered *a, b,* or *c* for each of the Eleven Keys.

Confidence
a. _____
b. _____
c. _____
- If most of your answers were *a,* you may have an inflated level of confidence.
- If the majority of your answers were *b,* your confidence is healthy.
- If most of your answers were *c,* you could possess a low level of self-confidence.

Curiosity
a. _____
b. _____
c. _____
- If you answered mostly *a,* you could be labeled as very curious or possibly even nosy.
- If many of your answers were *b,* you are relatively curious.
- If most of your answers were *c,* you are not really very curious.

Decisiveness
a. _____
b. _____
c. _____
- If you chose *a* answers, you may have a tendency to make decisions very quickly.
- If *b* was your primary choice, you have a balanced approach to decision-making.
- If you primarily chose *c* answers, you may suffer from indecision.

Empathy
a. _____
b. _____
c. _____

- If you chose *a* answers, you have a tendency to let empathy for others overrule your actions.
- If *b* was your primary choice, you probably balance well between empathy and business.
- If you primarily chose *c*, you may not be very empathetic.

Flexibility

a. _____
b. _____
c. _____

- If you chose *a* answers, you have a tendency to be overly flexible.
- If *b* was your primary choice, you probably show a balanced approach to flexibility.
- If you primarily chose *c* answers, you may not be very flexible.

Humor

a. _____
b. _____
c. _____

- If you chose *a* answers, you have a tendency to overuse humor in situations where it may not be appropriate.
- If *b* was your primary choice, you probably balance humor with being serious appropriately.
- If you primarily chose *c* answers, you may not use or appreciate humor often enough.

Intelligence

a. _____
b. _____
c. _____

- If you chose *a* answers, you have a tendency to rely most on thinking things through in situations that would benefit from intuition and emotion as well.
- If *b* was your primary choice, you probably balance intelligence with the other Keys.

- If you primarily chose *c* answers, you may not take an intelligent approach as often as you can.

Optimism

a. _____

b. _____

c. _____

- If you chose *a* answers, you may be overly optimistic and not acknowledge reality.
- If *b* was your primary choice, you probably react and behave optimistically in a balanced way.
- If you primarily chose *c* answers, you may have a pessimistic viewpoint more often than not.

Perseverance

a. _____

b. _____

c. _____

- If you chose *a* answers, you usually achieve goals and take action easily.
- If *b* was your primary choice, you balance analysis and introspection with action and persistence.
- If you primarily chose *c* answers, you may lack goal orientation, persistence, or follow-through.

Respect

a. _____

b. _____

c. _____

- If you chose *a* answers, you are described by others as professional and courteous.
- If *b* was your primary choice, you probably exhibit a mix of sensitivity and professionalism with impatience or abruptness.
- If you primarily chose *c* answers, you may be less sensitive and courteous to others than you could be.

Self-awareness

a. _____

b. _____

c. _____

- If most of your answers are *a*, your self-awareness is very astute and you could even manipulate others with your emotions and drives at times.
- If the majority of your answers were *b*, your self-awareness is quite balanced.
- If most of your answers were *c*, your self-awareness may be very deficient.

Now it's time to learn more about the Eleven Keys and how to use them to improve your communication and interactions with people at work.

Difficult People

Everyone has a bad day once in a while, but for those whom *every day* is a *bad day*, we have a polite name: "difficult." Every kind of workplace has a few resident difficult people with toxic personality traits and bad business habits. Their behavior ranges from poor listening, indecisiveness, and rigidity to erratic, insensitive, or even borderline psychotic behavior. It's tempting and very natural to want to avoid someone who offends or provokes you; however, wisdom and logic dictate that it's a better strategy to find a way to get along with them and become more immune to their particular "style" of doing business. Regardless of what interpersonal deficiencies people suffer, a connection can always be made using one or more of the Eleven Keys.

There are five general kinds of difficult people. They are listed below along with the Key(s) that the person is likely to be missing.

1. THE POOR COMMUNICATOR
Challenging Trait or Behavior:

Doesn't listen—You know this is a problem when you have to repeat yourself more than once or when the poor listener's reaction doesn't match your message appropriately.

Someone who doesn't listen may lack:

- **Respect** for others and their thoughts and perspectives.
- **Curiosity** about people, information, and ideas.
- **Empathy** for someone else's situation.

- **Self-awareness** about his inability to listen to other people.
- **Confidence**, yet appear to be overly confident.
- Or, **Flexibility**. If he's not interesting in changing, he may not see the point of listening to other's ideas.

Challenging Trait or Behavior:

Talks too much or constantly—The constant chatterer seems to talk endlessly about any topic and is usually repetitive as well.

A frequent or incessant talker may lack:

- **Confidence**, which can cause someone to overcommunicate or be repetitive and redundant.
- **Self-awareness**.

Challenging Trait or Behavior:

Interrupts others—This person barges into every conversation and cuts people off before they can finish their sentences.

Someone who interrupts coworkers in conversations, meetings, and on the phone may be:

- Overly **Decisive** and has already made up his mind about what to say or do next.

Or lack:

- **Respect** for other people's opinions or knowledge.
- **Curiosity** about anything other than his own perspective.
- The interrupter is certainly without **Self-awareness** of his troublesome communication habit.

Challenging Trait or Behavior:

Unresponsive—Someone who doesn't react or respond may often have a blank look on his or her face or, even worse, a catatonic stare.

Unresponsive individuals lack:

- **Confidence** about expressing ideas or opinions.
- **Decisiveness**—If someone doesn't speak up, he may be unable to make up his mind to express what he thinks or believes.
- **Curiosity.**
- **Empathy.**

Challenging Trait or Behavior:

Doesn't speak or write clearly—Listening to this person talk in meetings or reading his e-mails is torture! His words and thoughts aren't focused, persuasive, or succinct.

Someone who is an unclear and unfocused communicator doesn't possess:

- The **Flexibility** to communicate with different types of people.
- **Empathy**—a necessary ingredient for creating communication aimed toward the needs of others, rather than himself.
- **Confidence**—something successful communicators always have.

Additionally:

- An ineffective communicator rarely prepares, lacking an important element of **Perseverance.**
- A communicator who isn't clear is not in tune with himself, missing **Self-awareness.**

Challenging Trait or Behavior:

Complains or whines frequently—Nothing pleases this person and, even worse, she's not really interested in solving any of her problems.

A complainer or whiner lacks:

- **Optimism**, because they are usually so mired in a cycle of negativity that they don't know how to be positive.
- **Flexibility**, because change represents disaster for them.
- **Confidence**. People who are confident are realistic. Complainers are definitely not realistic because everything is miserable.
- **Respect** because a complainer/whiner is oblivious to how irritating his constant complaining is to others.

While some complainers and whiners:

- May use **Humor** as a tool, most do not, and can rarely lighten up and certainly can't laugh at themselves.

Challenging Trait or Behavior:

Nonverbal communication is negative or unappealing—This individual's body language and gestures often don't match his verbal message. Poor eye contact, a limp handshake, and fidgeting are typical signs of poor body language.

The inappropriate nonverbal communicator lacks:

- **Self-awareness**, a crucial Key for realizing the important impression that nonverbal communication makes on others. Without it, it is easy to misstep body language, gestures, and other types of nonverbal communication.
- **Confidence**.
- **Empathy**. A person who demonstrates inappropriate nonverbal communication may not realize that a successful communicator is always geared toward his audience rather than himself. **Empathy** is the Key that fuels this outward orientation.

Challenging Trait or Behavior:

Communicates emotionally—Constantly angry, upset, or sad, this person is rarely composed and manages to disrupt everyone else with his emotional tone or tirades. He becomes cynical, moody, or hostile when times are tough and shows frustration when resisted or blocked.

An emotional communicator lacks:

- **Respect.** Someone who is consistently angry, upset, or frustrated shows a lack of Respect for others because of the uncomfortable environment he or she creates.
- **Confidence.** Someone who cries, angers easily, or is overtly emotional usually lacks **Confidence**.
- **Humor** is a Key that can be used to defuse emotionally charged situations; people who rely on anger or frustration usually are unable to genuinely laugh at themselves or with others.

2. THE DISRESPECTFUL PERSON

Challenging Trait or Behavior:

Bullying—This individual usually holds an authoritative position that he uses to his advantage to yell at, pick on, or demean employees who are less senior to him. His communication can be inconsistent and erratic.

Someone who bullies others lacks:

- **Respect!**
- **Confidence,** because the only way he can make himself feel worthy is to make others feel meaningless or bad. A confident person doesn't need to put down others in order to feel good about himself.
- **Humor.** Bullies don't tend to be lighthearted and funny, although they can laugh at their victims.
- **Curiosity** about what matters to other people.

Challenging Trait or Behavior:

Poor etiquette—Someone who doesn't display manners or follow commonly understood formal and informal guidelines and norms of gracious behavior such as excusing oneself or saying "please" or "thank you."

Someone with poor manners is missing:

- **Empathy** for others. A large part of proper etiquette is focusing on others.
- The **Confidence** to believe that he can perform smoothly in every interpersonal situation.

Challenging Trait or Behavior:

Lack of integrity or ethics—Lying, cheating, stealing or deceiving other people to further his agenda are common behaviors in this category. Other behavioral indicators include a lack of trustworthiness, an inability to keep confidences and a tendency to misrepresent himself or his agenda for personal gain.

Someone who lies, cheats, or steals lacks:

- **Confidence**, because someone who relies upon illegal or unethical behavior doesn't believe in themselves.
- **Respect** for others, because people are usually hurt by unethical or illegal behavior.
- The **Intelligence** not to behave unethically, break laws, and go against norms.
- **Empathy** for the victims of unsavory behavior.

Challenging Trait or Behavior:

Disdain or apathy toward others—Doesn't understand the value of making others feel appreciated and/or respected. She can be dismissive or unsympathetic, doesn't give people recognition or praise, and doesn't do anything to nurture, help, or coach others.

Someone who is disdainful or apathetic toward others:

- Seriously lacks **Empathy** *and* **Respect** for others.
- Appears to be arrogant, pompous, or self-absorbed—qualities that seem to require a high level of **Confidence**. Indeed, the person appears overly confident, which is nearly always a mask for low **Confidence**.
- Views herself as the most important person in the world and has very little **Curiosity** about other people.
- Hasn't developed any sense of **Humor**.
- Seriously lacks **Intelligence** because she doesn't realize that her coworkers are instrumental to her success.

3. THE RIGID PERSON

Challenging Trait or Behavior:

Unyielding—This person is unwilling to compromise or make concessions.

An unyielding person is obviously missing:

- **Flexibility**. Along with this lack comes the words "No," "Can't," and "Won't."
- **Decisiveness** and **Confidence**—two Keys necessary for taking different approaches and undertaking risk.

Challenging Trait or Behavior:

Incapable of adapting or changing—Even when it's obvious that changing methods or behavior is necessary, this individual still drags his feet in favor of the status quo.

Someone who is incapable of adapting or changing:

- Clearly lacks **Flexibility**.
- Isn't willing to think about changing, and as a result tends to possess much less **Optimism** than someone who is.

- Doesn't have the **Decisiveness** to make choices to adapt or change.
- Doesn't possess **Intelligence**, because if he did he'd realize that most employers expect their employees to change at the drop of a hat.
- Has a low level of **Confidence**. Healthy **Confidence** is a necessary ingredient for changing.

4. THE NO-COMMON-SENSE WHEEL REINVENTOR

Challenging Trait or Behavior:

Lacks common sense with an inability to understand and use simple concepts or master habits, skills, and tactics for surviving and thriving—This person seems to be stuck in a cycle of "trial and error," and never learns from his mistakes or previous experiences.

Someone who is missing common sense:

- Doesn't have "street smarts" and therefore clearly lacks **Intelligence**.
- Doesn't have the **Curiosity** to learn how things work.
- Doesn't possess many of the elements of **Perseverance**, such as being motivated, persisting, and developing skills and habits to make things happen.

Challenging Trait or Behavior:

Unable to take a practical approach to solving problems and handling situations—His perspective and methods are often illogical and nonsensical.

Someone with the inability to take a practical approach to solving problems and handling situations:

- Doesn't exhibit **Decisiveness** or **Optimism** in coming up with applicable solutions and concrete outcomes.
- Lacks **Intelligence**, which is fundamental to handling situations and resolving problems.

- Lacks **Curiosity** about how other people have handled similar situations successfully.

Challenging Trait or Behavior:

Doesn't believe in or rely upon one's own intuition—Gut instincts aren't factored into her decision-making or problem solving.

When someone doesn't believe in or rely upon her own intuition:

- She definitely has a serious lack of **Confidence**.
- **Can demonstrate** an overuse of **Intelligence** because of an overreliance on facts or data.
- May lack **Optimism** and therefore distrust her instinctive hunches because she doesn't have faith that they'll be correct.

5. THE DYSFUNCTIONAL DECISION-MAKER

Challenging Trait or Behavior:

Makes poor decisions—Makes judgment errors when making decisions.

A poor decision-maker:

- Doesn't have the ability to gather enough information or the right information in the appropriate timeline; this is caused by poor **Intelligence**.
- Can absolutely lack **Curiosity** about how to make sound decisions.
- Naturally is missing **Decisiveness**!
- Doesn't tend to have a positive outlook, thus is missing **Optimism**.

Challenging Trait or Behavior:

Indecisive—Cannot make decisions easily or expediently, particularly under pressure, or he never makes a decision at all.

An indecisive individual:

- Can't make decisions at all or when under duress, so usually doesn't have **Confidence** in himself and his decision-making abilities.
- Is lacking an outlook filled with **Optimism**.
- Doesn't exhibit **Flexibility** about timing, working with other people, and gathering information.
- Doesn't know how to make things happen, which is integral to **Perseverance**.

Challenging Trait or Behavior:

Makes decisions too quickly—Instead of gathering the right amount of information or input, he leaps to a decision.

A hasty decision-maker:

- Overuses **Confidence** because he usually is convinced that he is right and doesn't need to consider other people's opinions.
- Also overuses **Decisiveness**.
- Moves quickly and typically will overuse **Perseverance**.
- Can even have too much **Optimism** about his decision-making prowess.
- May not have enough **Empathy** or **Respect**. He may disregard other people's feelings or situations in the interest of making a hasty decision.

A difficult person may possess one, several, or many of the traits within the five categories above. Regardless of how many bad business habits someone demonstrates, the reasons for their behavior can nearly always be tied to the Eleven Keys.

Now that you can see the connections between the Eleven Keys and someone's dysfunctional or annoying behavior, it's time to analyze a real person. Is there someone you work with right now who drives you crazy? If the answer is yes, it's probably easy for you to describe how this person makes you nuts. If you're lucky enough not to have a boss, coworker, or client who's difficult, remember someone from your past working life.

Write down a description of this person's challenging traits or bad behavior.

_____

_____

_____

What specifically does the person do that is difficult?

_____

_____

_____

How does it impact you?

_____

_____

_____

How does his difficult behavior impact your colleagues, department, or customers?

_____

_____

_____

How have you responded in the past to this person?

_____

_____

_____

What results did your approach have?

_____

_____

_____

What is your goal in dealing with this person?

_____

_____

_____

Perhaps he falls into one of the five categories listed above or perhaps you have identified a new behavior category.

Which Keys does this person need to develop or tone down? Refer to Part I: The Eleven Keys if you need to.

_____

_____

_____

Use this person as a case study to learn how to understand, tolerate, and get along comfortably with his or her behavior. Based upon the Keys you identified, go to the chapters—which are arranged alphabetically and numerically by Key—to learn more about each Key, how to handle the person, and how you can use the Keys in a balanced way.

Part II

USING THE ELEVEN KEYS TO GET RESULTS

Key #1: Confidence

Confidence is contagious. So is lack of confidence.
—VINCE LOMBARDI

Self-confidence—an unshakable belief in one's self based on a realistic understanding of one's circumstances—is a trait that most people admire in others and strive to acquire themselves. Confident people exude positive energy that draws others to them like a magnet. They tend to be optimists and risk-takers, and to excel at working under pressure, tolerating frustration, and coping with adversity. Confident individuals usually appear calm, relaxed, and "comfortable in their own skin." These are the people we all want to work with because their confidence is inspiring and becomes infectious.

Too much confidence, on the other hand, may cause people to delude themselves about the true nature of their abilities and to take unnecessary risks. It can also manifest in an arrogant, self-congratulating attitude. For this reason, working with an overly confident person can become tedious and annoying.

Most of us are born neither self-confident nor self-doubting, but we can very quickly take on either characteristic, depending on our early or past experiences and interactions with others.

When we are young, our parents' opinions of us play a critical role in our self-concept—the feelings and opinions we form about ourselves. For example, if your parents were critical, demanding, over-protective, or uncaring of you as a child, you may have begun to believe that you are inadequate, inferior, or incompetent as you grow up. Conversely, if your parents were encouraging, accepting, and loving, you probably had healthy confidence as you grew up.

Your friends' and teachers' opinions of you become a very powerful influencer of your confidence during your school years. Later, your confidence can be influenced by society, depending on how much focus you place on societal expectations and standards.

Confidence isn't necessarily a general characteristic that pervades all aspects of one's life. For example, Joan feels confident about her ability to relate to people but is not as confident about her athletic ability. Steve has no problem playing the saxophone in front of a live audience, but he gets nervous when he has to give a speech. Interestingly, confidence isn't always related to actual ability, but often mirrors *self-perception* and the individual's own *expectations* of him- or herself.

Why is working with a low-confidence person difficult? Take Bart, for example. Throughout Bart's childhood, his dad constantly communicated the message to his son that he wasn't good enough, smart enough, or athletic enough to succeed at anything in life. Now fifty-two, Bart still hears his father's critical voice in his head, especially when he experiences disappointment.

A year ago, Bart started a legal recruiting business. When Bart experiences difficulties negotiating deals with his clients, he often gives in to his low self-confidence and backs off, and is forced into less than fair agreements or loses the deal altogether. His clients don't particularly respect Bart, but they know he'll do anything they ask.

When you work with a person such as Bart whose confidence is low, your interaction with that person can be frustrating. He may be afraid to express opinions or take action, which can interfere with your ability to get things done when you must rely on him for information or if he's part of your team. A low-confidence person may put himself down or allow others to do so without standing up for himself. This kind of behavior creates tension and discomfort for everyone involved.

By the same token, working with an overconfident person can be as frustrating because people who openly demonstrate inflated confidence (sometimes called "hubris"), even if they have some ability or perform the tasks required of them, tend to come across as egotistical, arrogant, self-aggrandizing, or conceited—all qualities that most people find distasteful or unappealing. And yet, an individual who elicits such feelings in coworkers is unlikely to be voted the "go to" person to collaborate with on a hot project, or to be placed on the boss's short list for doing a make-or-break presentation to an important client.

The interesting truth about people who exhibit too much confidence is that, deep down, most are truly insecure. They tend to fantasize or deceive themselves about their true abilities in order to cover up or compensate for their low opinions of themselves, and to impress other people. Like the person who suffers from low self-esteem, the overly self-assured individual may need to take an honest look at his or her skills, talents, and abilities, take pride in those areas that are genuine strengths, and work on the ones that need improvement.

The rare person who truly is overconfident can be difficult to work with because they can lead you into risky situations that are hard to get out of, set you up for failure, and damage your reputation.

Healthy self-confidence tends to inspire trust and admiration, while overconfidence, whether real or not, can breed distrust, resentment, or even ridicule. Too little confidence may make others feel that they can take advantage of, overlook, or patronize the person plagued by this affliction.

POINTERS FOR WORKING WITH PEOPLE WHO LACK CONFIDENCE

Obviously, your tactics for handling someone's behavior will vary depending on the kind of relationship you have or how well you know each other. There are specific approaches for all levels of colleagues including peers, direct reports, and people who are senior to you (clients and customers are included in this category).

RELATED KEYS 〇━━

Key #1: Confidence

○━ **Curiosity** is a Key that enables you to learn, grow, and understand, which in turn gives you the Confidence to approach life's ups and downs armed with knowledge and perspective.

○━ **Optimism** is closely related to Confidence because it allows you to look at life through a realistic and positive lens. A hallmark characteristic of a confident person is one who is optimistic.

○━ **Decisiveness** is another quality of a confident person. Someone who makes rational and well-timed decisions, even when he doesn't have all the information, must be confident.

○━ **Perseverance** is fueled by Confidence. Often the reason someone doesn't make things happen is because of a serious lack of Confidence.

○━ **Self-awareness** is completely absent when one's Confidence is low. When someone's Confidence is healthy and balanced, his Self-awareness is also healthy and balanced.

The following will help you to pinpoint the people you work with who exhibit either low- or high-confidence behavior that in turn affects your ability to do your job, and some appropriate actions you can take to deal with that behavior.

LOW-CONFIDENCE BEHAVIOR

Someone chronically puts himself down or uses negative talk to describe himself.

If you are his peer: Ignore what he said and pay him a compliment; tell him that you are uncomfortable with hearing him always put himself down; or ask him to stop and say something nice about himself.

If you are his manager: Encourage him, compliment him on the things he does well, and show him that you believe in his abilities by delegating interesting or different tasks and projects.

If you are less senior: Smile, point out something he's accomplished recently or a trait he possesses that you admire.

Someone always avoids conflict, emotional situations, and disagreements.

If you are his peer: The next time a situation occurs that involves conflict or emotion and your coworker disappears, ask him if you can sit down with him and discuss what happened. If he doesn't want to talk about it, press the issue and reassure him by telling him that his involvement and input are important and necessary to you and everyone involved. Explain that his lack of involvement creates the perception that either he is a wimp or he doesn't care.

If you are his manager: Ask him to write out the steps for handling the situation; ask him for his input or suggestions for how to effectively handle such situations in the future.

If you are less senior: Ask him if he minds getting some feedback. If he seems open, tell him that employees would really appreciate his involvement in settling conflict and handling emotional situations. If he isn't open to feedback, ask him for advice about how to handle a specific difficult situation that occurred recently.

Someone seems reluctant to express opinions, especially in public.

If you are his peer: Tell him that you're surprised that he doesn't speak up in meetings since he has so much to contribute and you're sure other people would love to hear what he has to say. If he confides in you that he doesn't feel secure enough to talk in meetings, encourage him to start small by writing down something he can say before attending a meeting.

If you are his manager: Ask him to come prepared to talk about a specific topic at a meeting or even to lead it; ask him a leading question such as, "Sam, take a look at these statistics. Doesn't it look as if customer satisfaction is up this quarter?" You can explain that the perception that his colleagues have of him isn't just about the quality of his work, it also involves the way he communicates and whether or not he is confident enough to express opinions. Perception is reality.

If you are less senior: The next time you have a one-on-one meeting with this person, ask him if he thought the last meeting you attended together was productive. When he asks you why you are wondering about this, tell him that you really think it would add so much if he offered his opinions and advice in meetings.

Someone has a tendency to follow rather than lead.

If you are her peer: You can encourage her to take charge of something she feels very comfortable doing. If she doesn't know what this is, make some suggestions based upon your observations.

If you are her manager: You can put her in charge of a task force or team project, ask her advice about how to start a project you're involved with, or buy a good book on leadership and give it to her as a gift.

If you are less senior: Compliment her when you observe any leadership behavior she exhibits.

Someone discounts compliments and positive attention.

If you are his peer: You can tease him on how to gracefully accept compliments by saying "thank you"; compliment him regularly, in little ways, so he gets used to it; use gentle humor to show him it's OK to let yourself feel good about receiving a compliment or positive attention.

If you are his manager: You can use humor and compliment him and also tell him you'd like to coach him on how to respond positively and assertively when he receives any kind of attention.

If you are less senior: You can joke with him about his humility and the example he sets for others.

OVERCONFIDENT BEHAVIOR (Remember that this is usually behavior that a deeply insecure person exhibits to mask his low self-confidence.)

Someone behaves aggressively or dominates conversations.

If you are her peer: Tell her that you feel that she doesn't listen well; ask her politely to give you, or other people, a chance to talk; challenge what she's saying in a professional and respectful way.

If you are her manager: You can point out the ways that her poor listening skills affect her colleagues adversely.

If you are less senior: This is a tough one because this person could possibly have bully tendencies as well. The most effective behavior with someone this aggressive who outranks you is to show appreciation for his experience and position, share your concern for his agenda, and remind him of the business goal that you both share.

Someone is opinionated, a know-it-all, or a braggadocio.

If you are his peer: The know-it-all is usually competent and knowledgeable, but because he has little confidence, he needs to keep broadcasting that he is these things. Avoid competing with the know-it-all and let him know that you have heard everything he has said. Ask him where he did his research on the topic; nod and smile continuously; paraphrase what he says over and over again. Use softer language with this low-confidence person when introducing new ideas or information, such as "maybe," "perhaps," or "I may have an idea."

If you are his manager: Reassure him that his experience and skills are valued by the company. Ask him if he has any doubt that this is true. When he responds by saying he does feel valued or by asking why, this is your opportunity to ask him why he feels the need to broadcast his strengths. Tell him that his behavior makes others feel uncomfortable, and suggest that when he feels the need to brag or express his opinions, he write them down. Point out that his colleagues should be given the opportunity to express their opinions as well.

If you are less senior: Your primary goal with this person (other than immunizing yourself from his distasteful behavior) is to open his mind to your new idea or information so that he supports you. Always be overprepared, acknowledge whatever he's saying, introduce your idea subtly, and ask for his support, coaching, or mentoring. Never challenge him.

Since many of these behaviors are chronic or habitual, your responses will have to be repetitive until the other person gets the message. If tact isn't working, try being more direct. Ideally, it's best to sit with the person in a private area and describe, as tactfully as possible, how the low- or high-confident behavior makes you feel. Taking someone aside to have a frank personal discussion at work is not always possible, nor is it an easy thing to do. Even if your talk is effective for the moment, the other person may still continue to exhibit the offensive behavior. If that happens, you have a choice: Learn to live with it or, if possible, try to find another legitimate means of changing the situation.

Dave shares office space with Liz, who constantly interrupts him with her opinions when he's talking. Dave knows that Liz is really a nice person, but her behavior drives him crazy, sometimes to the point of rage. Dave figured out a way to handle the situation without hurting Liz's feelings: Whenever Liz would interrupt, he would resume his train of thought, exactly where he left off when Liz interrupted him, so that he sounded like a broken record. At first Dave felt silly doing this, but it worked. Now Liz doesn't interrupt him nearly as often as she used to.

People who exhibit annoying repetitive behaviors need to be dealt with repetitively, but with kindness and patience, until they break their annoying habits. It takes Confidence to do this.

A huge part of dealing with someone who has too much confidence or low confidence is for you to develop a healthy, balanced level of confidence.

ASSESS YOUR CONFIDENCE

Take the following assessment to help you decide whether you lack confidence, have too much confidence, or just the right amount.

Indicate how true each statement is for you by placing the appropriate number in the blank to the left of the statement.

5 = Definitely true
4 = Often true
3 = Somewhat true
2 = Rarely true
1 = Almost never true

_4_ 1. I really like and accept who I am.

_2_ 2. Usually I am able to not take mistakes or setbacks personally, and to view them as learning experiences.

_3_ 3. I never spend time thinking about how I can avoid looking bad or being embarrassed.

_4_ 4. I believe that I deserve the best that life has to offer.

_5_ 5. I can easily make a list of eight accomplishments in my work and personal life in the last five years.

_3_ 6. I express my opinions and feelings openly.

_2_ 7. I really trust my intuition or "gut" and follow what it tells me.

_4_ 8. I am able to visualize what I want or need and make it happen.

_4_ 9. I feel proud of myself when I overcome obstacles or improve something about myself.

_3_ 10. I am always conscious of how important my image (demeanor, appearance, and the way I act and communicate) is.

_4_ 11. I accept compliments graciously and without discomfort.

_4_ 12. I enjoy feeling successful.

_2_ 13. I have no trouble saying no to other people when I need to.

_ 14. I don't believe that others' perceptions of me are more accurate than my own.
_ 15. I do not need to be liked by everyone in my life at all times.
_ 16. My past does not influence my behavior and feelings.
_ 17. I don't often magnify the negative aspects of things.
_ 18. My behavior almost always reflects the way I feel inside.

SCORE KEY

Add up the numbers that you entered for each question. If you scored:

18 to 35—Your low self-confidence is probably negatively affecting many aspects of your life. It may make sense to seek professional counseling to understand why your self-assurance is so inferior.

36 to 54—You probably feel confident in some areas of your life and not so confident in others. While this is normal for many people, it could benefit you to focus on increasing your confidence in those areas that could use it.

55 to 72—You like and respect yourself and have learned to accept both your positive and negative qualities. Because you feel good about yourself, you tend to enjoy life.

If your score fell between 73 to 90, you may be too confident at times and not have a realistic outlook on yourself. People could view you as egotistical or conceited at times. It is possible that you aren't actually that confident and you cover this up by acting overly confident.

If your score fell between 55 and 72 and you feel comfortable with your level of confidence, you may want to focus on how to deal with other people who are either too confident or are not confident enough.

If you scored lower than you would like or fell into the too-confident category, the following assessments will help you to pinpoint some reasons you do and the behaviors you may exhibit.

NOT ENOUGH CONFIDENCE? COMPLETE THIS ASSESSMENT

Before you can learn how to boost your confidence, it is important that you understand how your low level of confidence affects your relationships with people at work. Ask yourself the following questions and write down your answers.

What areas of your life do you feel less confident about, and for what reasons? (Examples of areas: interpersonal skills, abilities or competence, appearance or image, intelligence or education, relationships.)

_____

_____

_____

_____

How does your low confidence level affect your relationships with your boss, colleagues, clients, and other people at work? Please give one example of each. Here's a model you can refer to in giving your answers: "I feel that Pete, my coworker, takes advantage of my inability to say no when he asks me to help him with tasks that aren't part of my job. Because of this, I avoid Pete, since I don't feel confident about turning down Pete's requests for help, unreasonable as they may be."

_____

_____

_____

_____

Typically, people who have low confidence exhibit many of the following behaviors: negative self-talk; avoidance of conflict, emotional situations, and disagreements; inability to express opinions, especially in public; a tendency to follow rather than to lead; discounting compliments and positive attention or behaving aggressively and being opinionated in an attempt to mask insecurities. Which of these behaviors have you shown recently? You may realize which behaviors you've demonstrated subconsciously, or because you've received feedback in the past. Write down the specific situation that occurred as a result of your behavior.

_____

_____

_____

_____

Frank is corporate counsel at Lisa's firm and attends many of the same meetings she does. It feels as if he disputes everything Lisa says, which causes her to retreat into her shell and stop talking. Is there someone at work who causes you to feel especially insecure or seems to take advantage of your low confidence? Who is this individual, and why does he or she make you feel this way? How exactly does he or she behave toward you? How do you respond? Write your answer below.

_____

_____

_____

_____

Do your answers help you to see more clearly how your low confidence affects your behavior at work with other people? If you were able to stop putting yourself down or to appropriately confront a supervisor or coworker who disagrees with you, you would probably already be doing this. The key to mastering these desirable abilities is to work at boosting your confidence. Now it's time to move ahead and complete some exercises that will help you improve your confidence and make your work relationships richer and more rewarding.

TIPS AND TECHNIQUES FOR IMPROVING YOUR CONFIDENCE

Choose from this selection of exercises designed to help boost your confidence level.

good wl Leah Ann

Give Yourself Credit for Past Effort and Successes

Write down two positive things that you've achieved in the last six months. Have you learned something new? Have you started a workout program or lost weight? Have you solved a problem that had been bugging you?

_____

_____

_____

Now, think about what you did to make your accomplishment happen. Did you adjust your attitude? Did you write down your goal and look at it frequently? Did you take a class, read a book, or ask someone for help?

_____

_____

_____

The purpose of this exercise is to remind you that you have recently been successful in making something good happen for yourself, and that if you've done it before, you can do it again. Applauding yourself for achieving something meaningful or desirable to you, no matter how simple, is a great technique for developing confidence.

Create a Positive "Incantation"

If you lack confidence, you may have a habit of using unflattering or overly critical words that you say to yourself either silently or out loud and that only make you feel less confident. An incantation is a simple phrase or group of words recited to produce a magical effect. In this case, the desired effect is bolstering your self-image. To help create your incantation, write down something negative that you habitually say to yourself about yourself, either out loud or in your head. Here's an example: Whenever Gwen forgets to ask her boss a question, she always tells herself, "I did something really stupid." If Gwen took time to think about it logically, she would realize that the idea of labeling herself "stupid" just because she didn't get all the information she needs from her boss is . . . well . . . ridiculous!

_____

_____

_____

Now, think of a positive phrase or motivating expression that has meaning to you, and write it down. In Gwen's case, she might write, "I want to be sure I complete my task as well as I can." The next time Gwen forgets to ask her boss something, she can say to herself, "I'm intent on doing the best job I can so I need to ask my boss more questions." Obviously, it's better if she uses her mantra to remember additional questions while she's still in her boss's office so that she doesn't constantly have to go back to him with rudimentary questions.

_____

_____

_____

The next time you catch yourself using negative self-talk, quickly substitute the incantation you've just written down. Doing this repeatedly will help you to develop belief in yourself, and create a new habit of positive self-talk. Gradually, this new habit will replace your old one, help connect your behavior, and help you to strengthen your faith in yourself.

Take a Risk

People with low confidence tend to shy away from undertaking new experiences because of their fear of failure. Learning to approach new experiences as opportunities to learn new things, rather than occasions to win or lose, is the key to positive risk taking. Think of something at work you'd like to do, something that you see as risky (which has prevented you from doing it). Do you want to network with a senior executive in your company? Do you want to volunteer for a task force? Do you want to make a presentation at an upcoming meeting? Whatever it is, write it down.

_____

_____

_____

Now, write down, step by step, what you have to do to make this happen. Try to keep it simple. Do you need to learn more about the thing you have in mind? Who do you need to talk with? What kind of preparation do you need to do? What about taking a class?

1. _____
2. _____
3. _____
4. _____
5. _____

Now that you've named the risky thing you'd like to do, and the steps needed to accomplish it, write down the three worst things you can think of that might happen if you take a risk and fail to achieve the results you were hoping for.

1. _____
2. _____
3. _____

Realistically, what are the chances of each one of these things happening? If it did happen, how would you, or someone you care about, be affected? Now, look at your answers and try to honestly assess how much they are based on your fear or on a logical assessment of the situation.

What Do You Like About Yourself?

Make a list of five things you like about yourself. Don't ask anyone else what he or she likes about you. Make this list on your own.

1. _____
2. _____
3. _____
4. _____
5. _____

What Do Other People Like About You?

Ask five people to tell you one thing that they like about you. If someone repeats an answer you've already received, ask for a different answer. Write the answers down.

1. _____
2. _____
3. _____
4. _____
5. _____

Are any of the answers the same as yours? If so, that's great because it confirms that what you already know about yourself is what others value about you as well. Now, write the entire list down on an index card, or put it into your PDA device. Whenever you are feeling less confident, go to a place where you have some privacy, pull out your list and read it out loud to yourself!

Complete the Overconfident Assessment

If you scored in the overconfident category on the assessment on page 45, complete the following exercise:

What areas of your life do you feel most confident about, and for what reasons? (Examples of areas: interpersonal skills, abilities or competence, appearance or image, intelligence or education, relationships.)

_____

_____

_____

_____

Phil dominates meetings by spouting his ideas and opinions, and rolling over anyone who tries to speak up. His peers laugh at him behind his back, have nicknamed him "Know-it-all Phil," and avoid him whenever possible.

How does your high level of confidence affect your relationships with your boss, colleagues, clients, and other people at work?

_____

_____

_____

Typically, people with inflated confidence exhibit many of the following behaviors: complimenting yourself out loud, in front of others; instigating conflict and emotional situations when people disagree with you; expressing opinions constantly, especially in public places; a tendency to take the lead and even be overbearing; initiating positive attention for yourself; behaving aggressively; blaming others when something goes wrong; being opinionated and demeaning others. Which of these behaviors have you shown recently? Write down the specific situation that occurred when you did.

_____

_____

_____

_____

Tone Down Your Excess Confidence

Choose from this selection of exercises to help you to maintain a healthy level of confidence and to change your behavior from egotistical to self-assured.

Most people who exhibit overconfident behavior may actually feel insecure, deep
down. Do yourself a favor. If you are reading this book, here's your chance to take a
quiet, honest look at yourself and your behavior. If you think you tend to come across to
other people as being overly confident or even arrogant at times, because you may be
compensating for a _lack_ of confidence, then the logical thing to do is to help yourself
feel more confident. If this is your situation, flip back in this chapter to page 45 and
take the assessment.

If you truly are overconfident, this assessment will provide you with a "reality
check" about how you affect other people, and what you can do to change your behavior so that other people will feel more comfortable around you.

Balancing Your Strengths with Areas You Need to Develop

List five of your greatest strengths.

1. _____

2. _____

3. _____

4. _____

5. _____

Now, list five areas in which you could use improvement.

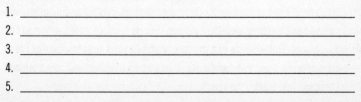

1. _____

2. _____

3. _____

4. _____

5. _____

GETTING FEEDBACK

If you took the assessment earlier, you read the list of behaviors that are characteristic of someone who is too confident. Now, read the list below and check off each behavior you think you may demonstrate at work:

___ 1. I compliment myself inappropriately in front of others.

___ 2. I instigate conflicts, emotional situations, and disagreements if people don't agree with me, or I feel I am not heard.

___ 3. I express my opinions constantly, especially in public places.

___ 4. I have a tendency to take the lead, even when someone else is the designated leader, and to be overbearing at times.

___ 5. I tend to blame others when something goes wrong because I always think I can do a better job.

Hopefully, you were able to be honest with yourself. If you think you may have been a little easy on yourself, go back and change your answers accordingly. Now, look at the numbers you checked. For each one, find the corresponding number on the list below, and read the suggestion for modifying that specific overconfident behavior.

1. Self-promotion is certainly a necessary element of succeeding at work. However, doing too much of it can make others feel as if you believe that you are better than they are. The next time you feel the urge to compliment yourself in front of other people, stop and think about your real purpose for wanting to do that. Is it to get attention that you feel you deserve but aren't getting? Is it to make you feel good about yourself because you secretly fear that you may not measure up? If you suspect that either of these things may be true, don't judge, scold, or put yourself down. But do try something different: Instead of saying the self-aggrandizing compliment out loud, write it down and read it to yourself.

2. Most people are very uncomfortable with conflict and will want to avoid you if you have a habit of creating it just to get attention. Conflict and disagreement can be healthy if they are legitimate and if those involved work together to find a resolution. But if the conflict stems from one person's need for attention, or as retribution for a perceived slight, it will be seen and felt by others as an attempt to manipulate them.

3. Do you express your opinions constantly, and in a pompous or superior manner, because you want people to think you are smart or well educated? If so, why are their opinions important to you? Usually, a person labeled by others as a know-it-all doesn't really know it all. Be cautious and thoughtful about trying to show people how much you know. Think how you would feel if you were on the receiving end. It may help to remember that the word "opinion" is defined in the dictionary as "a belief that is held often without positive knowledge or proof." Modesty is the sign of a confident person.

4. Even if you are a "born leader," it's inappropriate to designate yourself as the leader when someone else is in charge. This dominating behavior won't help you gain respect when you really are the person running the show. Respecting other people's roles is a sign of a healthily confident person.

5. Helping coworkers to become more involved, and to learn and develop themselves professionally, is a wonderful thing to do—if you are doing so in a genuine spirit of collegiality. People make mistakes, show poor judgment, and do shoddy work at times. Beating them up because of this is rarely a good technique for creating trust. And the fact that you think you could have done a better job is unimportant. Always focus on the positive aspects of someone's work before gently pointing out the negative facets.

CREATE AN ACTION PLAN

Changing your level of confidence requires time and effort. Writing out a simple action plan, and executing it, can help you to change your behavior. Organizing your plan into short, medium, and long time increments will help you stay on track. Here is Gwen's action plan, to use as an example:

My goal: To increase my confidence so that I can hold my own in meetings with my boss, handle difficult interpersonal situations more comfortably, and feel good about myself and about my abilities.

MY SHORT-TERM OBJECTIVES/ACTIVITIES:
1. Substitute my negative self-talk with my new motivational phrase, "I am good at what I do."

2. Call one person every week who cares about me, and ask him or her to pay me a compliment based upon my real strengths and positive qualities.

MY MEDIUM-TERM OBJECTIVES/ACTIVITIES:
1. Take a presentation-skills course by the beginning of June.
2. Join Toastmasters, a national organization that helps people overcome their fear of public speaking (toastmasters.com).
3. Network with two people in my industry whom I respect.

MY LONG-TERM OBJECTIVES/ACTIVITIES:
1. Write a research paper on my industry specialty, and send it to a few key people in my company and to all my clients.
2. Work on nurturing my relationships with my three most difficult clients.

Now, fill out your own action plan. Depending on your progress, your plan may change over time, but it's a good idea to start somewhere, to ensure that you will take seriously your goal of developing a healthy level of confidence.

My goal:

_____

_____

My short-term objectives/activities:

_____

_____

_____

By when: _____

My medium-term objectives/activities:

_____

_____

By when: _____

My long-term objectives/activities:

_____

_____

_____

By when: _____

There is a Hasidic Jewish saying, "The man who has confidence in himself gains the confidence of others." People with a solid level of confidence know that they are lovable and capable; this self-acceptance gives them the capacity to care about themselves and other people. They take sincere joy in others' successes and are saddened by their disappointments. Truly confident people don't feel the need to build themselves up by tearing other people down or by patronizing those who are less competent. They are assertive without being aggressive.

Healthy confidence is one of the most valuable assets a person can have, both at work and in life. Your confidence level reflects how you perceive other people and situations and can play a critical role in determining your success in every aspect of life. Of the Eleven Keys, confidence is one of the most difficult to learn and maintain, but without it, the other Keys can't be developed as easily.

Key #2:
Curiosity

*I think, at a child's birth, if a mother could ask a fairy godmother
to endow it with the most useful gift, that gift would be curiosity.*
—ELEANOR ROOSEVELT

Curiosity—the human need, thirst, or desire for knowledge—begins
at birth. Most children are naturally curious, instinctive explorers,
questioning and wondering as they learn about the world. According
to noted child psychologist Dr. Bruce Duncan Perry, if a child remains
curious, as she grows older, she will continue to learn and discover
new things.

Conversely, explains Dr. Perry, adults can easily stifle a child's curiosity by instilling fear, expressing disapproval, or being absent, either
physically or emotionally, from the child's day-to-day life. A child's
emotional, social, and cognitive development is expressed through
the quantity and quality of his experiences. If those experiences are
limited, he will make fewer new friends, join fewer social groups, read
fewer books, and be less active than the child with a robust sense of curiosity. The less curious child is harder to teach, inspire, and motivate.

Adults who retain a healthy sense of curiosity tend to be open-
minded, independent, alert, and observant. They are genuinely interested in other people as well as in a wide variety of subjects, and
are generally enthusiastic, even passionate, about life. Manhattan-
based psychologist Steve Axelrod believes, "Psychologically, there is a

link between curiosity and aliveness throughout the life cycle—curiosity is a basic function that renews and replenishes the sense of self."

Curiosity plays a big part at work because so many projects, tasks, and instances of communication involve dispensing information to and gathering information from other people. This requires asking questions, analyzing, researching, and being interested in every new person, experience, activity, and interaction with which you're involved. If you work with someone who isn't interested in these things, he usually doesn't tend to take the initiative to do things beyond his job description. A noncurious coworker certainly doesn't spend time trying to approach work creatively or solve problems in a different way because he is lacking the motivation to explore and discover. It's possible that he is also lacking the Key Flexibility. Someone who isn't curious about other people is someone who can be lacking interpersonal skills, particularly in work relationships, not to mention missing the Keys Empathy and Respect. It's awkward to work with someone who isn't natural at interacting with his coworkers, or who just isn't curious about the people he works with.

Fred and Roseanne were assigned to a task force to identify specific problems that were plaguing their department, specifically in the area of marketing. Fred and Roseanne each took a different approach to the assignment. Because the task force had nothing to do with his job, Fred spent very little time asking a few people outside the department some questions, scribbling their answers on a scrap of paper. Roseanne, on the other hand, identified ten people who were involved with the department and interviewed them, face-to-face and by phone, about the experiences they had with marketing and their perspective about the situation.

When Fred and Roseanne met to share their findings, they found, not surprisingly, that they had come to very different conclusions. They decided to test each of their conclusions independently before presenting them to their boss. Sure enough, Roseanne's thorough approach and genuine interest in learning about her interviewees' thoughts and experiences elicited feedback that was more meaningful and therefore more valuable to their boss than Fred's more superficial findings. Can you guess which one of these employees got the bigger year-end bonus?

Roseanne demonstrated the traits of a person with healthy curiosity, such as her ability to ask different types of questions, her empathy for others, and her interest in possibilities. While researchers have linked curiosity to productivity, growth, and healthy relationships, there has been scant investigation into the disadvantages of having too much curiosity. The expression "curiosity killed the cat" explains what we all know, that inappropriate or "negative" curiosity—better known as nosiness or meddling—is rarely appreciated by those who are its object. There are some important things to remember when making another person the object of your inquiring mind. Try to balance your inquisitiveness with caution, sensitivity, and respect for the other person's boundaries so as not to be perceived as intrusive. Ask questions, but don't interrogate. Pick the right time and place. And, above all, be aware that even with the best intentions, you still may risk making the other person uncomfortable by inadvertently crossing a personal threshold of privacy. Unfortunately, the overcurious coworker doesn't understand these guidelines and is someone that others just want to avoid.

POINTERS FOR WORKING WITH PEOPLE WHO ARE LACKING OR EXCESSIVE IN THE CURIOSITY DEPARTMENT

Here are some techniques for handling people who either exhibit a low level of curiosity or are overly inquisitive. When an employee reports directly to you, it's easier to encourage him to explore, learn, and understand more. If you're interacting with someone at work for whom you don't have direct responsibility but whose lack of curiosity is impacting your productivity, then you have more of a challenge on

RELATED KEYS O━━━

KEY #2: CURIOSITY

O━ **Confidence** and Curiosity are closely intertwined. Without Confidence, it can be hard to become curious, and without the knowledge and understanding that Curiosity brings, it's difficult to be Confident.

O━ **Optimism** is fed by Curiosity, and whatever you learn by being curious feeds Optimism as well.

O━ **Empathy.** Someone who possesses this Key must be curious about things besides him- or herself.

O━ **Perseverance** has a significant relationship to Curiosity. You can wonder about things all you want, but actually doing whatever it takes to turn your thoughts into action (e.g., making phone calls, following through on details) is what counts.

O━ **Self-awareness** is balanced when you are constantly curious about yourself. Curiosity isn't only directed toward other people.

your hands. It's also tough if someone senior to you doesn't have enough curiosity, especially when they affect your work.

LOW CURIOSITY

Someone makes decisions or takes action on a project you're involved with, and you're sure that he hasn't learned everything he can to get the best result.

If you are a peer: Ask him a series of different types of questions about how he came to his conclusion, so that you can identify where he may have fallen short in gathering information or understanding the situation. If he gets defensive, you can explain that you're concerned about realizing the best outcome for the project, not in judging his competence or abilities. You can question him this way whether or not you are his manager, however your language will have to be more subtle if you are coworkers.

If you are his manager: State outright that you aren't convinced that he has been thorough enough in his research, and explain specifically why this is so. As with any conversation you have as a manager, address the business outcome rather than the person himself. Ask him if you can see what his methodology was for gathering the information he needed to make a decision.

If you are less senior: Tell him that you respect his opinion or decisions, but you can't help feeling that he may not have had all the information he needed to make the decision. Reassure him that this is not a reflection of him, but that you and your teammates might not have been able to get all the data to him in time.

A colleague never asks questions when you delegate a task or assignment to him. Because of this, he often has to redo it (or you do).

If you are his peer: Often, it's necessary to delegate tasks and responsibilities, even to your peers. Realistic as this is, your coworker still may not be too thrilled that you have asked him to do something for you and, as a result, may not be very curious about how to do it the right way. If you suspect that this is the case, be careful to be as respectful as you can when asking him to handle the task. Explain why he is the best person to do the job (he has special talent or experience, etc.) and how you can support him when he's accomplishing the task.

If you are his manager: After clearly explaining the task you'd like done, ask him to paraphrase back to you what you've asked him to do, and ask again if he has any questions.

If you are less senior: Delegating upward can be touchy, but there are definitely situations that require you to do so. If this person habitually does a poor job with tasks or projects you ask him to become involved with, it could be that the person isn't curious enough to get the right information. It could also be that this person might have other priorities that he views as more important and will repeatedly put before your needs—not because this person isn't curious, just because he isn't curious about anything beyond his world. Asking him questions about his work may open him up to being more interested in other things (like your work). Also, be aware that it's up to you to learn and understand how this senior person prefers information to be organized and presented—especially if you want his help in the future.

Someone repeatedly argues with you or other people, is unresponsive, or becomes defensive instead of asking questions to try to understand the entire situation.

If you are his peer or his manager: Step back and look at yourself and the way in which you typically respond to the specific behavior. Are you locked into the same pattern of knee-jerk reactions every time with that individual? Instead of reacting the same way, stop yourself the next time and just ask questions and listen. What do you think is motivating the person to be angry or withdrawn? Once he has calmed down, ask him to communicate with you by asking questions instead of making statements. Keep encouraging him to communicate with you this way. Then schedule a time to meet and give him feedback about how his emotional (or nonemotional) reaction causes you and others to feel. Explain that this is a great technique for defusing emotionally charged situations and moving them to a reasonable, mutually acceptable conclusion. Note: Being argumentative or nonresponsive is not necessarily a sign that a person isn't curious. However, encouraging overly emotional individuals to redirect their energy into curiosity can help to pull them out of their emotional state and into a more effective and productive mode of work behavior. This approach can be used with someone regardless of whether they report to you or work as your cubicle mate.

If you are less senior: Ask him if you can sit down with him to discuss your business relationship. Tell him that you feel that your relationship isn't productive because of the pattern of behavior that constantly takes place between you. Ask him what his perspective is about this. If he gets overly emotional, and defensive or dismissive, tell him that you'd like to continue the conversation when he's feeling less angry (or whatever his emotion is). Explain to him that this was really hard for you to do but that you are interested in working effectively together so you were willing to take the chance. Because this is such a difficult conversation to have, write out a simple script before your meeting and practice saying it out loud.

TOO MUCH CURIOSITY

Someone is nosy, habitually asks inappropriate questions, or butts into other people's business.

If you are a peer: The next time he is inappropriately nosy, ask him to sit down with you as soon as you are able. Tell him that this incident made you very uncomfortable and explain why as clearly as you can by describing how it makes you feel when he asks intrusive questions. Explain that his behavior makes you want to avoid him and that you're sure that this isn't what either of you want. Try to give him specific examples of questions or topics that feel inappropriate to you.

If you are a manager: Sit him down and explain that this behavior is unacceptable and uncomfortable and that you'd like him to stop. The direct approach is probably the best way to handle an overly inquisitive person. Respecting someone's privacy at work is also an aspect of the Respect Key. Explain that no one feels comfortable being the victim of unwanted or malapropos attention, and ask the individual how he might feel if the tables were turned.

If you are less senior: It's difficult to tell anyone that his behavior is making you uncomfortable, especially someone who outranks you. Remember, though, just because someone does outrank you, this doesn't give him the license to make you feel ill at ease. The guidelines for having a conversation with a senior manager or client about his nosiness are similar to those for dealing with a coworker or subordinate. Point out a recent, specific incident that occurred, and explain why it feels unsuitable to you. Tell him that you know he will respect your feelings, and thank him for listening to you. If he's reasonable, he should take you seriously.

Someone has an opinion about you or someone else that is clearly inaccurate because she didn't take the time to learn all the facts and understand the full picture.

If you are a peer: Ask her to share her methodology and the information upon which she based her conclusion. Then, take a piece of paper and draw a line down the middle. Put her name on the left top and yours on the right top. Write down the information she shared with you in her column. In your column, jot down all the information (trying to stick closely to facts) that she didn't mention. Often, seeing this in print can help a person who tends to jump to false conclusions to realize that she should have made more of an effort to learn the whole story.

If you are a manager: Explain that one of the qualities of an employee that you admire most is the ability to come to reasonable conclusions based upon learning, understanding, and assessing information and situations fairly. Ask him to explain what his reasoning process was in the particular situation that caused you some concern. Once you've listened to his explanation, offer some suggestions and encourage him to increase his curiosity as well as his analytical skills.

If you are less senior: If the person with a misperception of you is your manager, immediately sit down and clarify what really happened. If it's someone higher up than your manager, ask your manager for help in clearing up the inaccuracies.

ASSESS YOUR CURIOSITY

Your ability to deal more effectively with people who demonstrate any of the behaviors listed above is directly related to how well balanced *your* curiosity is.

Take the following assessment to help you determine how curious you really are. Indicate the degree to which you agree with each statement by circling the response that best describes you.

1. I am very curious about a lot of things.
   Almost always   Sometimes   Rarely

2. I am constantly trying to learn something new.
   Almost always   Sometimes   Rarely

3. When I'm talking to someone else, I ask as many questions as I can.
   Almost always   Sometimes   Rarely

4. I love having new experiences.
   Almost always   Sometimes   Rarely

5. I tend to speculate about things rather than take them at face value.
   Almost always   Sometimes   Rarely

6. I really like having as much information as I can about anything I'm involved with.
   Almost always   Sometimes   Rarely

7. I rarely feel bored with life.
   Almost always   Sometimes   Rarely

8. I like to take things apart to see what makes them work.
   Almost always   Sometimes   Rarely

9. People who know me describe me as inquisitive and interested.
   Almost always   Sometimes   Rarely

10. I can easily make a list of ten things I'm really interested in.
    Almost always   Sometimes   Rarely

11. I like solving puzzles.
    Almost always   Sometimes   Rarely

12. I think I'd be a great journalist or private detective.
    Almost always   Sometimes   Rarely

13. I don't like it when I can't find the answer to something.
    Almost always   Sometimes   Rarely

14. I am usually willing to put myself outside my comfort zone in order to experience something new.
    Almost always   Sometimes   Rarely

15. I am equally interested in learning about people and information.
    Almost always   Sometimes   Rarely

SCORE KEY

Add the number of times you circled "Almost always" and multiply this number by 5. Write your score here: _____.

Add the number of times you circled "Sometimes" and multiply this number by 3. Write your score here: _____.

Add the number of times you circled "Rarely" and multiply this number by 1. Write your score here: _____.

Now, add all three numbers and write your total score here: _____.

55 to 75—You have a robust level of curiosity. You are typically open to and interested in knowing and learning about a variety of things. You are equally as interested in people as you are in things, information, and data. It is likely that you possess a healthy level of confidence because of your ability to approach new people and situations, regardless of any initial discomfort you may feel. Depending on where you fall on this

scale, you may at times even be considered by others to be a bit overly curious.

34 to 54—Your curiosity is piqued when you are naturally very interested in something or motivated to learn more. But when you aren't quite as interested, or you feel that someone else is imposing his or her own desire for information on you, you may tend not to extend yourself to learn about and explore the unfamiliar or unknown because you simply don't feel the need. Although this isn't necessarily a negative quality, research shows that curiosity and motivation are closely aligned, and that motivation is energizing. If you lack energy, this will impact your interaction with others at work.

15 to 33—If your score fell within this range, you may either be very bored or are just not an inquisitive person by nature. It's also possible that you have a low confidence level, which may prevent you from exploring the unknown. When you aren't curious, other people can sense your apparent boredom or indifference. Your attitude, whether in relation to your colleagues or to a project you're working on together, can make others perceive you in a negative light. Interested in changing that perception? Try making a conscious decision to learn something new—preferably something you've had a genuine or even passing interest in. Then begin your investigation. You may be surprised to find that what started out simply as an exercise in self-improvement may actually energize or motivate you, or even make you feel some passion for the subject you've chosen to learn about.

ASSESS WHAT YOU ARE CURIOUS ABOUT

This assessment will help you to determine some of the situations, topics, and areas that tend to pique your curiosity. Check the questions that describe something you are curious about or interested in if your level of interest is *average or stronger.* If you're just mildly curious about what the answer is, then don't check the question. Try not to spend too much time on each question.

_____ How many left-handed golfers have won major tournaments on the PGA tour?

_____ What motivated John Kerry to run for president in 2004?

_____ Why would someone want to appear as a guest on *Jerry Springer*?

_____ How many forts are standing in the United States today?

_____ How many people in the world collect orchids?

_____ How is a computer virus or worm designed?

_____ Why is Mick Jagger still touring?

_____ What are the primary reasons that business leaders fail?

_____ What are the most common causes of death in women under sixty-five years of age in the United States?

_____ Which are the top three performing hedge funds in the world?

_____ What are the qualities of a successful negotiator?

_____ What motivates your boss?

_____ What makes your boss angry?

_____ What is the per capita income in South Dakota?

_____ Which organization has the best customer satisfaction rating in the retail industry?

_____ What are Netflix's annual sales?

_____ What is considered to be the premier audio company, according to audiophiles?

_____ How long did it take to invent Microsoft Word?

_____ Why are some people organized and others not?

_____ What would it be like to teach a class?

_____ How does someone learn to appreciate opera?

_____ Where did the CFO of your company grow up?

_____ How many Web sites are there in the world?

_____ How difficult is it to drive an eighteen-wheeler truck?

_____ Why do people have children?

_____ How much money does a rodeo star earn?

_____ How does a ventriloquist throw his voice?

_____ What five new products introduced to consumers were the biggest flops last year?

_____ What are the five hottest industries right now?

_____ How many reality TV shows have aired in the last five years?

_____ How does someone build a ship in a bottle?

_____ What is the annual budget for your company's marketing department?

_____ What is the leading cause of death in Egypt?

_____ Where is Azerbaijan?

_____ How many U.S. prisoners are sitting on death row?

_____ How many people work as accountants for U.S. companies?

_____ What does a horologist do?

_____ How many meetings have you attended in your adult lifetime?

_____ How does someone change careers?

SCORE KEY

Add the number of questions you checked. If you scored:

28 to 40—You are enormously curious about many different things. It's likely that you truly enjoy discovering, exploring, and learning, and you display your curiosity both in your work and in your interpersonal relationships. You tend to take risks and rarely, if ever, feel bored. Your natural curiosity gives you the capacity to amuse yourself even when you're alone, because you never have trouble finding something to keep your mind occupied. At work, you are known as a self-starter.

15 to 27—Your level of curiosity is generally contingent on whether or not you are motivated to find out more about a given subject. Your motivation to learn something new tends to be externally driven, say by an assignment you've been given by your manager. Or it can spring from feeling too much inertia or boredom.

1 to 14—You are rarely, if ever, curious. Rather than seeking out new people and experiences, you prefer to remain in your comfort zone. Your lack of curiosity may be inhibiting you from developing and enhancing yourself, both professionally and personally, and from enjoying mind-broadening and enriching experiences. It may also discourage others from approaching you with new ideas or interesting opportunities, or from soliciting your help in solving problems.

Now, take a few minutes to review the questions you've checked. Is there a common theme among your selections? If your score indicates that low curiosity may be holding you back from succeeding at work, you may need to think about the real reasons for your lack of interest and inquisitiveness. Are you just bored or are you really depressed? Are you suffering from burnout? Are you unwilling to put in the effort to explore new areas because of laziness, or could you be in real need of a change in your work situation?

If you scored between 15 and 54 on the first assessment on page 67, and between 1 and 27 on the assessment you just took—then keep reading. The next section of this chapter will give you the opportunity to complete some exercises that can help you to improve your curiosity.

TIPS AND TECHNIQUES FOR IMPROVING YOUR CURIOSITY

Choose from this selection of exercises designed to help you increase your curiosity level. You may select a few exercises or complete them all. If you work with someone who needs to improve his curiosity and is open to changing, any of these exercises will help him increase or balance his curiosity, too.

What Can You Learn in Your Job?

If you work in a specific functional area such as finance, marketing, information technology, or human resources, you may have frequent exposure to or interaction with other departments. If you work for a large company, there may be other divisions or companies with which you have limited contact, but which you could benefit from knowing more about. As anyone with a successful career will tell you, a large part of career success is contingent upon getting to know as many people as possible within your organization and, more important, letting them get to know you. The more curious you are at work, the more you'll interact with others because you'll ask questions in order to solve problems and then you'll be able to contribute more ideas and solutions. Doing so will have positive implications on your work relationships and how you're perceived by your colleagues.

Chris, twenty-seven, has been working in the same customer-support role for two years and is a bit bored. A billion-dollar company with many divisions recently acquired his company, and Chris decided to learn more about what other job opportunities might exist for him within the larger corporation. He was savvy enough to tell his boss what he planned to do, and fortunately she was supportive. Using the online company directory, Chris made a list of all the department heads and of the human resource professionals who supported each department. He updated his résumé to reflect the work he'd done for the last several years, then systematically called or e-mailed everyone on his list, requesting an opportunity to meet with them to learn more about the organization and about any possible current or future job openings in their departments. Everyone Chris contacted was so impressed by his initiative that they went out of their way to meet with him and to educate him about their area of the organization.

Chris is now in the enviable position of having to decide between a marketing manager spot and a product development position. Not only did Chris use Curiosity to explore and understand his company, he also used Intelligence and Perseverance to his advantage. In addition, he has developed some high-level relationships within his organization that will be invaluable as he advances in his career, even if he eventually leaves the company.

Think about your organization for a moment. Write down the name of a department or division that you know very little about but would like to learn more about. Maybe you're not sure which areas of your company you'd like to learn about, so why not pick the department you know nothing about? Chris identified product development and marketing simply because he had no idea what they did.

_____

_____

_____

Next, write down three or four questions that you'd like answers to.
Examples may be: What exactly is product development responsible for accomplishing? How does it fit into the company as a whole? What kind of experience do people in this department have? How does product development in this industry compare to product development in other industries?

_____

_____

_____

_____

_____

Thinking about what you'd like to learn can be fun, but committing to actually doing it is what can really change your life. Write down the name of every person you need to contact in order to get the answer to your questions, along with his or her phone number and/or e-mail address. Next to this, write the date by which you plan to contact that person. Because networking is a crucial business skill, buy contact-management software such as Act! or Microsoft Outlook and enter all the names and numbers of the people you meet into one database.

_____

_____

_____

_____

Sometimes we aren't curious enough about the people and things closest to us. So many people work for companies without any idea of how the company is structured, how many employees work there, what the annual sales figures are, and other facts that may help them to become more knowledgeable, well-rounded professionals.

THE ART OF ASKING QUESTIONS

Knowing how to ask questions, and carefully—or actively, rather than passively—listening to the other person's response, is a skill that many people don't have. But that doesn't mean it can't be learned! The ability to ask the "right" questions—that is, questions that are likely to reveal the information you're looking for—is perhaps the most important aspect of curiosity. It can also help you to understand what is at the crux of a difficult person's behavior.

There are many different kinds of questions you can ask. Below you'll find a few types of questions and their definitions. After reading about them, you'll have a chance to practice writing down your own sample questions and to use them in a real situation with someone at work. Asking questions can be a valuable tool to use when you're involved in a conflict with a colleague, or when you're uncomfortable or uncertain about the possible motive behind another person's behavior. Questioning is also a nice way to let people know that you are interested in them or that you care about them.

TYPES OF QUESTIONS

The Fact-Finding Question

One of the most straightforward types of questions, the fact-finding question, is used to elicit factual information, or a simple yes or no answer. This kind of question is also called a "close-ended" question because the possible responses are cut-and-dried. Here are some examples of fact-finding questions: "Did you e-mail the report to Joe on Tuesday?" "What time did you send it?" "Has he responded yet?"

Unfortunately, many people ask more of this kind of question than any other because it's the easiest kind to ask. It's unfortunate because a close-ended question, as its name implies, can be a kind of dead-end if you really need more in-depth information from the other person.

The Open-Ended Question

Unlike its opposite, the "open-ended" question generates conversation, leaving room for the respondent to express emotions, motivation, and intent, and also to give details. Examples include: "How do you think we should handle this?" "Why do you feel that's an important detail for us to know?" "What was your impression of the sales manager we just met with?"

The Thought-Provoking Question

This kind of question is asked to elicit creativity, new ideas, or a different perspective. It can stimulate the respondent to think "outside the box." Check out these examples: "How would you approach this project if you didn't have any resources?" "What if we added another shift?" When asking this type of question, sometimes it's a good idea to warn the person that you want to ask an unusual question in order to look at a situation or problem from a different perspective, so that he or she won't think you are merely being provocative.

The Comprehensive Question

This type of question, which has several parts, requires a complex or multipart response. It can be useful in situations where there's a lot of information to transmit, understand, and digest. Notice that this example combines fact-finding and open-ended questions:

- "When exactly do you want to launch the new product?"
- "What's been getting in your way?"
- "Why do you think that's happening?"
- "Specifically, what have you done to overcome these obstacles?"
- "What do you plan to do next?"
- "How can I support you?"

Think of a situation at work involving another person that is complicated or unresolved. What additional information do you need to obtain in order to bring it to a conclusion? Describe the situation.

_____

_____

_____

Whom do you need to talk to or meet with to exchange or gather information?

_____

_____

_____

Now, using the four types of questions listed above, write down one question for each category.

Fact-Finding

_____

_____

Open-Ended

_____

_____

Thought-Provoking

_____

_____

Comprehensive

_____

_____

Now, it's time to put your questions to the test! Send everyone on your list an e-mail, or leave a voice-mail message, to arrange a time to ask your questions. If you think that a face-to-face meeting, as opposed to a phone call or e-mail, would be the most effective way to elicit the information you need, then say so in your message.

Let's review three basic, far-reaching benefits that you can reap by developing your curiosity. First, if you express your curiosity in a positive way, other people will feel flattered that you're interested in them and will appreciate the effort you're making to understand them and their situation. Second, being more curious about yourself and about the ways you affect others can help you to navigate more successfully in today's ever-changing, complex workplace (see Key #11: Self-awareness). And finally, gathering as many kinds of information as you can—not just facts and figures, but subjective, anecdotal stories that reveal people's thoughts, feelings, and motivations—can help you to gain better control of your work, particularly if a difficult person or situation is involved. Keeping yourself stimulated by learning new things, taking a class, reading a self-help book, listening to an instructional tape, or playing a CD or DVD—whether it's of personal interest to you or purely for professional development—can do a lot to "juice up" your healthy curiosity.

ARE YOU TOO CURIOUS?

This next section is for you if you've ever been accused of being overly inquisitive or downright nosy. Nobody likes a busybody. It feels intrusive, obnoxious, and rude to have someone prying into your personal business or asking questions that "cross the line." If you were overly curious as a child, it's likely that adults giggled nervously when you asked a nosy question but quickly quashed you and your snooping.

You may not really be nosy, yet you may be known to have a tendency to "beat a dead horse" by asking far more questions than a situation may merit. If so, ask yourself, "Why do I need to do this?" Could it be that you have an excessive need to gather as much information as possible to make a relatively simple decision? Is it because your confidence is low? Or do you use perseverance to a fault by persisting too much? If these are possible reasons for your "over the top" behavior, then be sure to read about Key #1: Confidence, Key #3: Decisiveness, and Key #9: Perseverance to learn how to work on these three specific Keys.

Janelle is self-employed as a consultant and, like most business owners, has good months and not-so-good months, financially speaking. Once every three months, she has breakfast with her friend Parker. Janelle adores Parker and often uses him as a sounding board to discuss some of the issues she faces in her business.

But Parker does one thing that makes Janelle so uncomfortable that she could scream—he asks her how much money she thinks she'll earn this year. She finally had to spell out for Parker that she finds this line of questioning incredibly nosy. Parker was surprised by Janelle's comment because it never occurred to him that his inquiry about Janelle's finances could be perceived as anything but normal and inoffensive. Soon after Janelle's confrontation with Parker, there was a bit of discomfort between the two friends, but now things are back to normal, and Parker doesn't ask Janelle about her income anymore.

Sometimes, simply thinking about the questions you're planning to ask someone, *before* you do it, is the easiest way to avoid behaving inappropriately or coming across as overly inquisitive. Another approach is to imagine how you would feel if someone asked you a question about a topic that you deem extremely personal. This is where the Keys Empathy and Respect can be helpful.

CREATE AN ACTION PLAN

Unlike some of the other Keys, increasing your level of curiosity isn't that difficult to do. Staying curious, however, is a taller order. Just as for every Key, writing out an action plan is an easy way to help you identify where you need to beef up your curiosity or, if you happen to fall into that small group of busybodies, tamp it down a bit.

Felicia is a bit bored at the moment in every aspect of her life. She suspects that she comes across this way to others and feels ready to try to undo her bored state by learning something new. Here is Felicia's action plan, to use as an example:

My goal: To shake myself out of my bored state by learning some new things, both personally and at work.

MY SHORT-TERM OBJECTIVES/ACTIVITIES:

1. Sign up for a kickboxing class at the new gym that just opened in my neighbor-hood. (Physical exercise is always stimulating.) By when? Next Friday.
2. Start keeping a journal to document my life so that my (future) children will be able to read about my thoughts and experiences. When will I begin? Tomorrow.

MY MEDIUM-TERM OBJECTIVES/ACTIVITIES:

1. Read and throw away the stack of trade publications sitting on my desk. By when? Within three weeks.
2. Get to know the new vice president of finance by inviting him to lunch and nurturing a relationship with him. When? I'll e-mail him tomorrow. Take a class on the new regulations in my industry. When? I'll do research on what's available and enroll in the next three weeks.

Felicia's action plan is fairly short-term, but yours doesn't have to be.

Now, fill out your own action plan. As is usual with most action plans, yours may change over time, but at least you'll get it down on paper.

My goal:

_____

_____

_____

My short-term objectives/activities:

_____

_____

_____

By when: _____

My medium-term objectives/activities:

_____

_____

_____

By when: _____

My long-term objectives/activities:

_____

_____

_____

By when: _____

Throughout our lives, most humans have a natural inclination to form relationships and embrace new experiences that will lead us to a better understanding of where we fit in the grand scheme of things. That's what curiosity is all about. Once you begin to focus on being appropriately curious, you will notice a difference in your relationships and your work overall. Your healthy curiosity about your coworkers will cause them to want to trust you and want to work with you. Your curiosity about ideas and how to improve the way you work will motivate and energize your colleagues, even those who are difficult.

Key #3:
Decisiveness

In a moment of decision, the best thing you can do is the right thing. The worst thing you can do is nothing.
—THEODORE ROOSEVELT

In today's high-tech, high-speed world, the ability to make rapid decisions is an essential skill at work. But while speed is important, knowing how to render sound judgments is the ultimate test of a true professional.

Decision-making is a popular topic in books about leadership. Most business decisions involve people. If the individual in charge is chronically paralyzed by indecision, the people whose job performance depends on his or her ability to make up his or her mind will flounder in a sea of ambiguity and uncertainty. The quality of their work—not to mention their morale—will suffer.

Gary Klein, author of *Sources of Power: How People Make Decisions,* interviewed firefighters, nurses, and other professionals whose jobs demand the ability to make on-the-spot, life-and-death judgments. Klein learned that even with the need to make immediate decisions, emergency workers either compare pros and cons based on facts or go with their gut instincts. The real key to effective decision-making, he says, is to make a choice and stick with it, even if that choice may turn out not to be the best one. It's the method used to arrive at a decision that is important, in Klein's view. The ideal decision-making process involves a combination of two elements: comparing the pros and cons, and listening to your instincts.

Fortunately, most of us are not routinely called upon to make actual life-and-death decisions at work—although sometimes it may feel to us as if the opposite is true. Even so, being prepared to make decisions at a moment's notice is the mark of any skilled professional or entrepreneur in today's unpredictable and ever-changing business world.

Why do many people have difficulty making decisions? There are a slew of reasons. Do any of these apply to you or your coworkers?

- Avoidance of responsibility
- Fear of change
- Reluctance to take risks
- The need for acceptance and approval
- The need to avoid confrontation
- Apathy
- Being a perfectionist

A decision in and of itself is virtually meaningless. Why? Because the whole purpose of decision-making is to take action of some kind, even if this means deciding not to act. Kit has started four projects in the last six months, and her manager has begun asking her when she is going to complete them. Kit knows that she needs to move ahead and make some decisions, but what's holding her back is the knowledge that once she makes some choices, she'll have to take action on her decisions. For Kit, implementing her decisions has always been daunting, so stalling final decision-making is her coping mechanism.

The chronically indecisive person often sends a message that he or she is insecure, wishy-washy, or afraid of taking chances. A person who possesses these traits is tedious to deal with because he is always second-guessing himself and, in the process, is preventing you from getting your job done.

If your manager is indecisive or makes poor-quality decisions, this is frustrating to you and your teammates because rightfully you expect him to be a critical thinker and problem-solver, to be sensitive to and respectful of your time, and to take appropriate action when the situation demands it. His failure to demonstrate these skills will contradict and eventually undermine your trust in him as a leader.

No matter what someone's role is, his approach to decision-making is a direct reflection of his ability to problem-solve; think clearly, critically, and creatively; identify opportunities; and commit to a course of action. And action, ultimately, is what decision-making is all about!

Michelle started a new job in human resources. One of her first assignments was to review and revise several policies to ensure that they were meeting the letter of the law. After completing her policy review, Michelle was required to run it by Peter, an attorney in the legal department, who had to "sign off" before the revised policies could go out to everyone.

It's been three years since Michelle came on board, and the policies are still not revised. Why not? Here's what's been happening. When Peter receives the policies from Michelle for his review, he makes minor changes—usually unrelated to his field—and sends them back with the request to have an opportunity to review them one more time after the changes he suggests are made. Whenever Michelle honors his request, Peter either changes the policies back to their original form, makes more non-value-added changes, or doesn't respond at all.

Too late, Michelle has learned that she is the third person to be assigned this project and that her two predecessors were equally unsuccessful in getting Peter to move on it. Not only has Peter's indecisiveness been incredibly frustrating to Michelle and a waste of her valuable time and energy, she gets written up by her boss in her annual performance reviews for not completing the assignment, despite the fact that her boss is well aware of Peter's contribution to the problem. Apparently, indecisiveness is a way of life in Peter's department. His boss jokes openly about the organization being at risk because of its out-of-date policies. "I know I should assign someone else to review them and would," she says laughing, "were it not for the fact that I keep changing my mind!" But the joke may ultimately be on her if the company is slapped with a legitimate lawsuit by a disgruntled client or employee.

Just as bad as a chronic nondecider is a compulsive decision-maker—a person who consistently makes snap decisions with minimal or no forethought, analysis, or input from others. The drive to make rash decisions can result in mistakes, negative consequences, and even offending the very people who should be involved in the decision-making process! Ironically, although the rash decision-maker may at first give the impression of being a strong leader, the habit of handing down decisions that consistently reap subpar results, or do real damage, may reveal a personality riddled with deep insecurity, anxiety, and an inability to understand the often "gray" aspects of a situation.

Peggy was the executive director of a small nonprofit that provided services to the homebound elderly. When a well-intentioned board member told Peggy that he was planning to make a large donation to the agency, Peggy immediately decided to announce the gift in the organization's newsletter, which was about to go to press. Well aware of Peggy's impulsiveness and that the board member in question was kindly but prone to making grand promises he couldn't always keep, Stephanie, the agency's development officer, and Susan, its public relations director, cautioned Peggy to hold off until the check was in the bank and the funds cleared. True to form, Peggy ignored their advice, the announcement went out, and the board member was furious. He denied ever having made the promise and resigned in a huff. Peggy, as well as Stephanie and Susan, earned a stiff reprimand from the board. Initially, Peggy's embarrassment made her contrite. But her contrition was short-lived. To make matters worse, she seemed oblivious to the negative impact her bad judgment had on her colleagues. Tired of feeling that they had no say in important issues that affected their job performance, Stephanie and Susan eventually both resigned, and Peggy lost two dynamic and loyal staff members.

RELATED KEYS 🔑

KEY #3: DECISIVENESS

🔑 **Confidence.** If you feel a basic sense of confidence in your mental abilities, intuition, and knowledge of the situation and subject matter you're dealing with, then chances are you won't be thrown when the need arises to make a decision and stick with it.

🔑 **Curiosity.** Any worthwhile decision-making process requires researching and analyzing a situation or problem by looking at such variables as the history, timing, people involved, available resources, and the possible pros and cons of taking a particular action. So Curiosity is right up there on the list of must-haves for a wise decision-maker.

🔑 **Flexibility.** Staying flexible can save you from reverting to old habits, attitudes, and ways of interacting with others that could blind you to possibilities and prevent you from discovering potential solutions.

🔑 **Intelligence.** The ability to take an efficient and "smart" approach can give you the courage to experiment with a new style of decision-making. This can be especially useful if the way you've made decisions in the past hasn't always been ideal.

🔑 **Perseverance.** Since action is the whole point of decision-making, Perseverance, the ability to hang in there until you've found the answer, is crucial every step of the way, including that final all-important step of putting your decision into practice.

🔑 **Self-awareness** plays a large part in decision-making, especially if you are paralyzed, because it allows you to look inside yourself to truly understand the reasons you are struggling with in making your decision.

POINTERS FOR WORKING WITH PEOPLE WHO LACK DECISIVENESS OR ARE TOO DECISIVE

Undoubtedly, you have to work with other people who are either indecisive or overly decisive. Here are some techniques for handling people at both ends of the spectrum, to make your life easier.

INDECISIVE PEOPLE—HOW DO YOU WORK WITH THEM?

It's reasonable to ask your direct reports to make decisions and to give them deadlines. It may not be as obvious how to assist your peers, your manager, or others who have seniority over you in making timely decisions in the areas that affect you and your work.

Someone rarely or never makes a decision on time, preventing you and your coworkers from moving forward in your work.

If you are a peer: Be sensitive and warm in your demeanor toward the person. Don't push her or demand a decision. Doing so will only exacerbate the person's indecision. Instead, open up a dialogue with the person about the situation, and discuss the pros and cons of each choice. Essentially, walk the person through the decision and the different outcomes, making the point of explaining why timeliness is of the utmost importance or particularly sensitive in this case. Once you've discussed the optimal outcomes and the best way to achieve them, help the person come to a decision and reassure her it is the best one.

If you are her manager: While you certainly can coach your direct report to use the same decision-making model described above, you have the added advantage of being able to set expectations with her before she has to make the decision. If the employee has worked for you for any length of time, you've already observed that thoughtful and expedient decision-making is hard for her. Because poor decision-making has several root causes, it's up to you to learn why it's tough for this employee. Is it low Confidence, inflexibility, a lack of the Key Intelligence, minimal Curiosity, or limited Self-awareness? This book is filled with exercises for each of the Eleven Keys. Once you've pinpointed which Keys your employee lacks or exaggerates, you can create a development plan with her using as many as makes sense.

If you are less senior: When you report to a poor decision-maker, it feels like your work life is constantly out of control, or in a holding pattern, because you're so dependent upon your manager or senior executive's decisions to get anything done. While it's likely that part of you resents having to "play psychologist" and analyze why your boss can't make decisions, it's always a great starting point to understanding dysfunctional managers. Read the list of Eleven Keys to determine which ones contribute to why your boss can't make decisions. Next, try to make every decision easier for this person. Is the information he needs communicated and organized the way he likes it? Are you or your coworkers readily available when he has questions or concerns? Push him a little bit every time he needs to make a decision that involves you or your department.

Someone makes decisions impulsively without involving you or other people.

If you are a peer: If you are one of the people routinely left out of this individual's decision-making process, approach him directly. Tell him how you feel when he decides something without your input. If this overly decisive person is a know-it-all, chances are he's a "control freak" with limited tolerance for ideas that he may perceive as contradicting or challenging. If this is the case, then it's doubly important that you come to meetings well prepared, with carefully thought-out ideas and new information to contribute. Keep documentation of this. Caution: Be careful to avoid using adversarial language with this person. Ask him questions as if you are looking for advice, even if it makes you grimace inside. If he is able to realize that you are not a threat, he may begin to solicit your input. But remember, no matter how careful you are, you are ultimately unable to control how another person perceives you, especially if he has a strong need to be in control.

If you are his manager: Ask him to identify specific checkpoints during a project or complicated task when he should schedule time with you to inform you of the decisions he's made and the decisions he plans on making. If he has made a rash decision without consulting you or other colleagues, ask him to explain his rationale for doing so, and emphasize the importance of checking in with you before making these decisions in the future. A rash decision-maker can be overly confident, impatient, and unable to be analytical or visionary, or simply is not collaborative. Ask him to help you to understand what is at the root of his rash decision-making behavior. Once this is clear, you'll be able to work with him to help him change his behavior.

If you are less senior: Someone in a leadership role may make quick decisions without consulting his direct reports or colleagues simply because he believes he knows what's best. If you report directly to this person, you and your teammates might approach him to discuss the fact that you don't feel as if you are part of a team when he does this. And also ask that in the future you are clued in so you can answer questions that may come up about his decision. If you sense that he doesn't care about this, then perhaps you could point out the repercussions of your team not being informed or "in the loop" on the decision-making process.

Someone makes a decision and then changes her mind over and over again.

If you are a peer: Manage this person's flip-flop decision-making behavior by honing in on her feelings. Her need to constantly change her mind may spring from her even deeper need to please other people. She may lack self-confidence or simply may be unsure of what to do next after she has made a decision, so she retreats into her comfort zone of inertia. Since she is most likely driven by the unrealistic desire to get along with everyone, she may be unable to see the potential negative repercussions of frequently changing her mind. Creating an open and trusting relationship with this chronic "people-pleaser" can be key to helping her stop vacillating. Once you have established trust, ask her if you can coach her through her decision-making process, and ask for commitments from her every step of the way. If it annoys you to think about the amount of time and effort you'll have to put into helping your flighty colleague stick with her decisions, remember how annoying it is to watch her constantly changing her mind.

If you are her manager: Encourage your employee to adapt some kind of decision-making model to use every time she has to make a decision. Every time she wants to change her mind about a decision she's made, suggest this simple decision-making process:

- Write down in detail the actual issue or problem that requires a decision.
- Write down all the decisions that need to be made. Next to each decision, write down the positive implications of the decision and anything that can backfire as a result of the decision.
- Give equal time to listening to your gut instincts and analysis of the facts involved.
- Make your decision and stand by it.

As with the other Keys, it's important that you are balanced in your ability to make decisions so that you can work easier with your colleagues who are not and ideally help them to be better decision-makers.

ASSESS YOUR DECISIVENESS

Take the following assessment to help you determine how decisive you really are. Indicate the degree to which you agree with each statement by circling one of the answers below it.

1. I am usually very decisive.
   Almost always   Sometimes   Rarely

2. There is hardly ever a time in my life when I'm struggling with some kind of decision.

   Almost always   Sometimes   Rarely

3. When I have to make a big decision, I use a specific decision-making model to help me.

   Almost always   Sometimes   Rarely

4. I am willing to take risks in order to make the right decision.

   Almost always   Sometimes   Rarely

5. When I need to make a decision that will impact other people, I don't think it's necessary to get total consensus from everyone involved.

   Almost always   Sometimes   Rarely

6. I am usually successful at using a blend of practical, creative, and critical thinking to make decisions.

   Almost always   Sometimes   Rarely

7. I always look at the root of a problem first before deciding how to handle the symptoms.

   Almost always   Sometimes   Rarely

8. The process used to make decisions is more important than the consequences as long as it's well thought out.

   Almost always   Sometimes   Rarely

9. I use a different approach to decision-making each time, depending on the circumstances and the nature of the decision I am required to make.

   Almost always   Sometimes   Rarely

10. I feel comfortable helping indecisive people make decisions.

    Almost always   Sometimes   Rarely

SCORE KEY

Add the number of times you circled the answer "Almost always" and multiply this number by 5. Write your score here: _____.

Add the number of times you circled the answer "Sometimes" and multiply this number by 3. Write your score here: _____.

Add the number of times you circled the answer "Rarely" and multiply this number by 1. Write your score here: _____.

Now, add all three numbers and write your total score here:_____.

41 to 55—You have great decision-making prowess. You consistently show sound judgment and sensitivity to other people's time and input. You realize that making the best possible decision is important, but that you must be prepared to take risks as well as responsibility for potential mistakes. If your score fell on the high end of this range, it's possible that you make decisions too rapidly, at the expense of other people.

25 to 40—You move back and forth between making decisions quickly and well and being indecisive. While this is normal for many people, you could benefit from developing consistency in your decision-making. Next time you find yourself wavering or delaying in making a decision, try to step outside your situation and analyze what makes this particular decision more difficult than one that wasn't so challenging for you. Do you struggle more with personal decisions than you do with professional ones, or vice versa? If so, think about why this is so.

10 to 24—Making decisions is a struggle for you, most or all of the time. Take a look at what causes you to stall or avoid making decisions. Could your lack of Confidence be the problem? Are you overly concerned about making the wrong decision? Are you worried about what others will think of you? Do you feel uncomfortable when you don't have enough information or the unanimous approval of others? Whatever the reason, it's time to work on improving your decision-making skills!

If you scored between 41 and 55, you are probably a great role model for those who struggle with making decisions. If you have a colleague who could use your coaching in this area, you may want to continue reading the next section of this chapter, which is for people who need to develop better decision-making skills. If not, go to page 86 for practical tips on how to deal with indecisive or overly decisive people.

Do you err on the side of being too quick to make decisions? If you do, completing the exercises on pages 98–99 in this chapter can help you to be a more thoughtful decision-maker.

If you scored between 10 and 39, the next section will provide you with exercises to help you conquer your indecision.

DEVELOP YOUR DECISIVENESS

Why Do You Have Trouble Making Up Your Mind?

Just as with any developmental task, an inability to come to a reasonable conclusion or judgment after sensibly weighing the facts and possibilities of a given situation often stems from a more deep-seated problem. This self-assessment will help you to determine what typically blocks you from making expedient and wise decisions. Think about a decision that you would like to make or one you've recently made but only after a struggle. In the space below, first describe the problem or situation. If you have already made a decision, describe, step by step, the process you used to finally arrive at your decision. If you have not yet made a decision, list all the factors and variables that you need to consider to reach a reasonable decision.

_____

_____

_____

Now, being honest with yourself, write down all the obstacles that are preventing you from deciding what to do. If you have already made the decision, what were the things that kept you from making the decision easily?

1. _____

2. _____

3. _____

4. _____

5. _____

How many of these obstacles are objectively real and how many are merely important in your mind? Read the list below and check your reasons for not making a timely and comfortable decision.

___ a.   I am afraid that I will make the wrong decision.

___ b.   I can't seem to get consensus from the people involved in the decision.

___ c.   I am afraid that other people will be unhappy with my final decision.

___ d.   The decision isn't really important to me; it's someone else's priority.

___ e.   I don't have enough information.

___ f.   I'll have to do something once I make a decision.

___ g.   I'm not confident about my ability to make the right decision.

___ h.   I'm too distracted by other people's opinions.

___ i.   I'm not really sure why I haven't made a decision.

Now, read the information that corresponds with the reasons you selected.

a.   When you're worried about making the "wrong" decision, ask yourself, "What is the worse possible thing that can happen if I make the wrong decision?" Now, think of some extreme responses. Will the wrong decision cause an illness or death? Will it cause bodily harm to someone? Will it cause someone to lose his or her job or self-respect? Will it make you feel humiliated? If you answered any of these questions in the affirmative, then you may need to spend more time reflecting upon, and involving others in, your decision-making process. The likelihood of any of these things happening is probably slim.

b.   If you are unable to get consensus from everyone who will be impacted by your decision, ask yourself, "Is consensus truly necessary?" "Are there specific people from whom I must get agreement and others whose opinions are not as crucial?" "Who are they?" "What are the real reasons people aren't giving their agreement?" "How significant are these reasons?" Once you've satisfied yourself with the answers to these questions, you'll feel much more comfortable making a decision.

c.   As the saying goes, "You can't please everyone all the time." While you may prefer to be well-liked and popular, sometimes you just won't be able to make everyone happy, especially if you are in a leadership role. If you think that your decision is going to displease people, clue them in beforehand that you are leaning toward making a decision they may not be happy with, and tell them why you've come to that conclusion. Check in with them once more after you've made your decision.

d. All of us have "stakeholders" in our professional and personal lives. Obviously, if your boss would like you to make a decision about something that *you* don't find important, it's probably a good idea to make the decision anyway. You may find it helpful to try to learn what your boss's underlying motive is for asking you to make the decision. If the decision is something that someone else wants you to make, *no matter who they are,* think hard about the possible consequences of *not* making the decision.

e. People who make rash and impulsive decisions don't usually have enough information because they are mostly interested in "making something happen." However, if you suffer from "analysis paralysis"—the need to have as much information as possible before making a decision—sit back and ask yourself why. While reflection and analysis are two essential ingredients for sound decision-making, overthinking a problem can interfere with the other key component—taking action to solve a problem.

f. Knowing that you must take action as a result of a decision you've made may be intimidating or unappealing. Does the action you have decided to take seem difficult, uncomfortable, or distasteful to you? Is there a way that you can break it down into manageable pieces? How about just starting with a few minutes a day, until you complete the dreaded task or project? Are there portions that you can delegate? Or is it something that you don't know how to do or have limited experience with? If you answered yes to the last question, then call or e-mail someone who has more experience than you, and ask for his or her advice on how to tackle the problem.

g. If confidence is an issue for you, read about Key #1: Confidence. Think about why you lack the self-confidence to make this decision. Being decisive is one of the hallmarks of a confident person, and building self-confidence is actually part of the cure for chronic indecisiveness. Taking a risk by making a well-thought-out decision, even if it turns out to be an imperfect one, is a great way to start building self-confidence.

h. Sometimes it's much easier to sit back and listen to everyone else's opinion about what you should do. While there are many credible and experienced people who can give you advice, there comes a time when you must draw the line and decide how many others you will consult before making your decision and sticking to it.

i.   If you really have no idea why you haven't made a decision, then perhaps it isn't a decision that needs to be made at all! Or, it's possible that you are unaware of, or "out of touch" with, what is really important to you in this particular situation.

TIPS AND TECHNIQUES FOR IMPROVING YOUR DECISIVENESS

If you are frequently indecisive, the reasons you are wracked by indecision probably fall into a pattern. The following assessment should help you to zero in on the most typical reasons for your indecisiveness so that you can catch yourself from falling into the same trap in the future!

LEARN A DECISION-MAKING MODEL

Sometimes the easiest way to become more decisive is by making decision-making a habit. One way to do this is to learn a simple model for decision-making and to use it every time you're faced with the need to decide. Start with a small decision first so that you can become comfortable with the model. Eventually, it will become second nature. There are many decision-making models to choose from. Here is a simple one:

Step One—Identify the specific problem and write it out in one or two brief sentences. Know the difference between a problem and the *symptoms* of that problem.

Example:

I am always late in submitting my monthly report to my boss. This makes my boss angry because *his* boss gets irritated. I need to decide how to fix this!

Step Two—Gather as many facts and opinions as you can from the individuals you rely on in making your decision. Use the same list of questions for everyone involved.

Example:

Did you know that I deliver my monthly report late to my boss every month?

What exactly do you do to contribute to my monthly report?

What do Mike, Susan, and Alfredo do to contribute to my monthly report?

Why do you think I am always late in getting the report to my boss?

What do you recommend I do to be on time?

Step Three—Develop several solutions for the problem and list them.
Example:

Try generating the report without Mike's involvement.

Give Mike, Susan, and Alfredo deadlines that are actually three days before the real deadline.

Ask my boss to extend the due date of the report by four days.

Change the content or format of the report so that it is simpler and easier to compile.

Step Four—Select the best alternative solutions by thinking it through.
Example:

Mike really needs to be involved with the report because his department is crucial.

Giving Mike, Susan, and Alfredo false deadlines isn't ethical.

Extending the due date would be nice, but I still have a deadline.

Simplifying the report is the best solution because, after investigating the problem, I've learned that my boss really only cares about one piece of information on the report.

Step Five—Get feedback from the people who are affected by your decision.
Example:

Mike, Susan, and Alfredo are very happy because I've cut their workloads in half where this report is concerned. As a result, they are far more cooperative and always get the information to me on time.

My boss is ecstatic because he always has the report in hand when his boss asks for it.

Finally—always, *always* listen to your gut! If there is a little voice in your head telling you to do something, pay attention to it first, *before* relying on your rational mind.

This decision-making model is a foolproof aid for sound decision-making. It won't guarantee that you'll make the right one every time, but it will definitely help you become a more skilled and confident decision-maker.

FAST DECISION-MAKING TIPS

Sometimes you may be called upon to make quick decisions without the benefit of using the decision-making model just described. Here are some techniques for making decisions under pressure:

- When it's a decision that isn't too important, such as, "Should I go out to lunch or eat in the cafeteria?" think about doing the opposite of what you normally would do. If you almost always go to the cafeteria, envision going out and trying the new sandwich shop you drive by every day.

- When you are having trouble making a decision and your deadline is fast approaching, promise yourself that you will make up your mind within two hours of waking up the next morning. Take a piece of paper and write down the decision you need to make. Put the paper next to your bed. Read it immediately when you get up the next morning. Why does this work? It's rare for someone to actually describe a decision that needs to be made on paper. Also, the instant reminder that it's a priority is very motivating.

- A decision that involves only you and can't affect or harm other people can be made with the simple flip of a coin. For example, if you are trying to decide between checking your e-mail and listening to your voice mail, flip a coin. If you feel disappointed by the coin's face, then simply do the opposite thing. Voilà, your decision is made!

DO YOU MAKE DECISIONS TOO QUICKLY?

If you tend to make decisions rashly, without taking into account the possible repercussions of your habitually hasty judgments—keep reading! There's nothing wrong with making decisions quickly. What *is* wrong is making decisions so fast that the outcome of your decision creates problems for you, your company, and other people. Unless you are in a profession or position that requires the ability to make split-second, life-and-death decisions, using time to your advantage will make you a better, and wiser, decision-maker. Even if you feel comfortable making an immediate decision, try using this simple decision-making model *before* you commit to a choice that you may end up regretting. Slowing down to think through your options prior to jumping in with both feet will help you to avoid looking back later on the results of your blunder and thinking, "If only I had taken more time . . ."

The Decision

What is the decision to be made?

_____

_____

Key Stakeholders

Who are the key stakeholders and how much do they need to be involved so that they can "buy in" and support my decision (especially if something goes wrong later)?

_____

_____

_____

Time Available

How much time do I realistically have to make this decision?

_____

_____

Importance of the Decision

How important is this issue or problem to the people I work with?

_____

_____

Information Needed

Who besides me has information or expertise that can add value to the quality of my decision-making process?

_____

_____

Building Trust and Credibility, and Developing People's Talents

Is there potential value in using this decision to create trust with others at work, enhance my credibility, or help my colleagues or staff to develop their talents in this area?

_____

_____

It should only take a few minutes for you to answer these questions. At the very least, you'll benefit from having taken some time to think through your decision instead of acting impulsively. If you answer these questions honestly, you may realize that it could benefit you to slow down your decision-making at times. Taking that little bit of extra time up front can only enhance your ability to make wise judgments. Think of the time you may save in the long run as a result of the potential errors in judgment you may have caught. What's more, you may even earn new respect from your colleagues and clients, and a reputation for being a calm and thoughtful decision-maker. A win-win situation, don't you agree?

CREATE AN ACTION PLAN

Since there are so many reasons why you may be indecisive, your action plan should be very specific. Focus on the aspects of decision-making that tend to trap you most often. As was noted earlier in this chapter, decision-making can become a healthy habit with repetition and practice. Marta has had difficulty making decisions as far back as she can remember. After reflecting on what prevents her from making up her mind, Marta determined that she has a habit of asking everyone she knows for his or her opinion, putting her own opinion last. Marta also realized that she is a people-pleaser. She is so concerned about what other people think of her that she subconsciously avoids making decisions so that she won't disappoint anyone. Here is Marta's action plan:

My goal: I am going to start making decisions confidently and efficiently without relying so heavily on everyone else in my life.

MY SHORT-TERM OBJECTIVES/ACTIVITIES:

1. Write down the last four decisions I've made at work. Replay the results of each decision in my mind, and analyze how important other people's advice really was to the outcome.
2. Develop a plan for building my Confidence from the ideas in the chapter on Key #2 so that I can feel more comfortable making decisions on my own when I need to, without any input from others.

MY MEDIUM-TERM OBJECTIVES/ACTIVITIES:

1. Identify and learn to use a decision-making model each time I must make an important decision. Create a template and make copies so that it is readily available for me to use.
2. Ask Carmen to coach me on decision-making. I've watched her. She is really good at making expedient decisions while gaining the collaboration of her coworkers and creating a climate of trust. And she seems so confident!

MY LONG-TERM OBJECTIVE/ACTIVITY:

1. Volunteer to chair next fall's big promotional event, run by my department, so that I am faced with dozens of decisions. It will be scary but exciting, and I'll be ready to rise to the challenge!

Now, fill out your own action plan. Doing this will be easier than you think, because you are faced with the need to make decisions every day. Whether these decisions are large or small, putting a plan together will help you to become more comfortable in your role as a decision-maker.

My goal:

_____

_____

My short-term objectives/activities:

_____

_____

_____

By when: _____

My medium-term objectives/activities:

_____

_____

_____

By when: _____

My long-term objectives/activities:

_____

_____

_____

By when: _____

The ability to make sound, timely decisions is fundamental to your relationships with the people you work with and to your overall success at work. If you've read this chapter, then you know the good news: Decisiveness is a habit—a skill that can be learned. Next time you're feeling plagued by indecision, or by the impulse to relieve yourself of temporary anxiety by jumping into a rash decision that you may later regret, consider the wise words of author Carlos Castaneda: "Worry and think before you make any decision, but once you make it, be on your way free from worries and thoughts; there will be a million other decisions still awaiting you."

Key #4:
Empathy

*. . . to think always in terms of other people's point of view,
and see things from their angle . . . may easily prove to
be one of the building blocks of your career.*

—DALE CARNEGIE, *HOW TO WIN
FRIENDS AND INFLUENCE PEOPLE*

Empathy is the ability to recognize and respond appropriately to another person's situation or feelings. The empathetic individual makes a
sincere attempt to understand the other person *from that person's point
of view*, and has a keen sense what it's like to "walk in their shoes."

The word "empathy" derives from the Greek word *pathos*, or "feeling." Empathy is different from sympathy, though people often confuse
the two. To have sympathy for another person is to recognize that they're
in pain or distress and to feel sorry about it. Sympathy can sometimes
be construed as condescending because "feeling sorry" for another
person can make you feel, or appear to feel, that you are in a superior
position to them. By contrast, being empathetic means that you identify
with and feel the other person's pain or distress as if it were your own.

The opposite of empathy and sympathy is apathy, a complete lack
of caring or interest in the other person's feelings. (Apathy can also be
a sign of burnout or a reaction to extreme stress.)

Most people are either born with or develop empathy at an early
age. As very young children, we learn to respond with sensitivity to
the feelings of our parents and siblings, other children, and even our

pets or other animals. Although there are always exceptions, generally speaking, parents who fail to model empathy raise children whose behavior toward others is a reflection of this.

FOOD FOR THOUGHT

Gender can play a role in empathy. A study by psychologist Steven Stein found that women, on average, are more aware of their emotions, show more empathy, and are more adept at interpersonal relationships. The research showed that men, on the other hand, are more self-confident, are more optimistic, and handle stress better than women. The good news is that both men and women can boost the emotional abilities they are lacking, whether it is Empathy or any other Key.

RELATED KEYS 🔑—

Key #4: Empathy

🔑 **Confidence** is important to possess in order for you to concentrate fully on someone else.

🔑 **Flexibility** shows the need to relate to ideas, situations, or feelings that may not always be yours.

🔑 **Optimism** goes hand in hand with Empathy. If you aren't able to take on a positive perspective, you will be unable to empathize fully.

🔑 **Respect** is all about sensitivity, courtesy, and professionalism. These are behaviors that are directed toward another person while empathizing.

🔑 **Curiosity** about someone's situation or plight is what fuels someone's ability to show Empathy.

🔑 **Self-awareness** is the ability to recognize your own feelings and emotions. An inability to do this means it's virtually impossible to show Empathy toward others.

POINTERS FOR WORKING WITH PEOPLE WHO LACK EMPATHY

Regardless of how empathetic you may be toward others, you can be sure of one thing: Somewhere along the line, you will encounter someone at work who will fail to show empathy toward you just when you need it the most.

Someone rarely or never shows concern for your feelings, but tends to focus exclusively on work or on himself.

If you are a peer: Think about how your colleague's lack of empathy makes you feel. Once you've identified those feelings, ask him politely if you can schedule some time to talk. In your discussion, be direct. Tell him you'd like to give him some feedback, and ask him to stop and listen to your perspective about how his self-centered, business-only behavior makes you feel. If he interrupts, or tries to change the subject, tell him again, politely, that you'd appreciate his undivided attention so that you can relate the information you'd like to share. Try to avoid showing overt emotion while you're having this discussion. Be prepared to repeat this tactic each time you encounter his off-putting behavior, which he's likely to have difficulty stopping, even if he's motivated to do so. Try to find an area in which he seems naturally to be able to show empathy.

Lisa had worked with Laura for three years, and Laura was always insensitive to her anytime Lisa experienced difficulty. Recently, Lisa's pet greyhound died, and much to her surprise, Laura oozed empathy for Lisa. All this time had gone by and Lisa never knew that dogs were a soft spot for Laura.

Often people who appear to have little or no empathy for others actually are quite vulnerable themselves. Whenever the nonempathetic person at work shows signs of having a problem or difficulty, be it personal or professional, make a point of showing empathy toward him. While this may be difficult to do at times, it's a strategy that can be very effective in breaking down the defenses of a nonempathizer and in helping him to bring out his human side.

If you are his manager: Make a genuine effort to get to know your direct report. What motivates him? What does he care about? What is his personal life like? When you've gained his trust, you can begin to coach him to be more empathetic toward you and his coworkers.

If you are less senior: If your manager or someone in senior management isn't empathetic, it goes without saying that it could just be his personality or that he may be focused only on business. Have you observed that he is empathetic toward his children or wife or certain people in the company? If so, perhaps you can bring it out in him by being empathetic toward him.

While it is hard to change someone who isn't empathetic, what's important in this situation is that you feel more comfortable around him. While you shouldn't change who you are, especially if you're very empathetic toward your coworkers, you can match your style to his a bit more closely. If you manage people and observe that he isn't very empathetic toward them, it's OK to champion them. It's never going to be comfortable working with a boss who isn't feeling toward others, but the important thing is to put the relationship in perspective—after all, it's business and business doesn't require that relationships are empathetic, only respectful.

Someone tends to be overly concerned with your or other people's feelings or emotions, to the detriment of business or herself.

If you are a peer: Tell her how much you admire her empathy toward others. If you have a trusting relationship, tell her that you've observed that her high level of empathy for others sometimes interferes with business. Ask her if she is aware of this, and offer to help be her "eyes and ears" in this area.

If you are her manager: Explain that her high level of empathy is greatly appreciated and rare in the business world. Then tell her that you're concerned that her ability to "walk in the other person's shoes" sometimes overrides the need to make decisions and take action that may not always be ideal for everyone, but are best for business. Encourage her to read about Key #3: Decisiveness. It may help her to learn how to develop and use a consistent decision-making model, which takes all variables into account.

If you are less senior: It is more common than you may think to work with someone who allows his empathy to overrule his business sense. Many larger corporations tend to beat overempathetic managers to death so that they become so weary that they leave. However, there are many smaller, privately held businesses that allow their managers to be too soft with their employees, which can jeopardize business results. If you do report to someone who needs to "toughen up," it's important for you to constantly remind her of the quantifiable business goals that the company expects. Often, a tender manager can lose focus of these in the interest of caring for her people. Complimenting her on her empathetic nature and then giving her behavioral examples of how her empathy has troublesome long-term effects is a strategy that you can take.

EMPATHY CAN BE LEARNED

It's easy to become desensitized at work. There is no profession where empathy is more critical than medicine. Yet psychological studies have shown that during medical school and residency, where the emphasis is traditionally on diagnosis and treatment with little attention paid to the patient as a person, many medical students begin to lose their ability to empathize with the pain and distress of their patients. How can a doctor build trusting relationships with the people he or she is supposed to be helping without being able to identify with their pain or discomfort?

There is a remedy. A new way of practicing medicine called "narrative medicine," developed by Dr. Rita Charon, teaches medical students how to be better listeners by using the story of the patient's illness, combined with traditional medical practices, as a way of understanding, diagnosing, and treating the illness. Since listening is crucial to empathy, the students are asked to listen to their patients and write stories about their illnesses. The process of absorbing and interpreting the patients' individual stories moves the students on an emotional level and makes them better caretakers.

Narrative medicine is a wonderful illustration of the fact that "everybody has a story to tell." But you don't have to be a doctor to benefit from learning to listen to and understand the stories of the people with whom you interact in business or at work.

EMPATHY: THE HEART OF A HEALTHY WORKPLACE

Medicine is not the only profession where the ability to listen and "feel for" other people is valuable, and even essential. Empathy is one of the five major building blocks of "emotional intelligence." Emotional intelligence involves abilities such as being able to motivate oneself and persist in the face of frustrations; controlling impulse; regulating one's moods; having hope. The other four building blocks are knowing one's emotions, managing emotions, motivating oneself, and handling relationships.

In today's world of constant change, downsizing, and globalization, a person's EQ, or emotional intelligence quotient, can be just as important, or more important, than his or her IQ. As any recent survivor of a corporate downsizing will attest, empathy in the workplace is in short supply and is needed now more than ever. Psychologist Michael Rock tells it like it is: "A workplace without empathy is a workplace that is sick, unhealthy at best, and very raw, uncaring, and vicious at worst. When we begin *not to care about* the people we work with, we also begin to act in ways that, unless corrected, lead to unethical activities . . . today, as never before, managers and employees need to be tuned in. Interpersonally, this means being able to 'emotionally read' other people. If you find that you are short on empathy, stop and think about how you might be more sensitive to people, especially those closest to you. Make it obvious to those around you that you want to establish good relations, and demonstrate thankfulness and appreciation."

Sadly, the typical workplace of the twenty-first century is cold, harsh, and even abusive. Look at Ike's experience. Ike recently quit his job as a senior communications director at a health maintenance organization that had gone through a rapid succession of mergers, to work at a hospital as a speechwriter and publicist. First on his list of criteria for a new job was "to work for senior executives who were sensitive and caring." He tells a story about an executive at his former workplace who came in and, on her first day, ripped all the photos of the previous leaders off the wall, exclaiming "It's a new world now, and you don't work for these old companies anymore."

There are things you can do to quash this kind of toxic behavior such as really listening to angry people, reminding yourself that someone's bad behavior usually has little to do with you, and extricating yourself from painful situations.

It's definitely possible to overuse empathy. Take Cheryl, for example. Her small, entrepreneurial employer was bought by a foreign bureaucratic behemoth. Overnight, the company's "fly by the seat of our pants" culture and management style was replaced by e-mails, faxes, and interminable conference calls. Cheryl still loved her job, had an amazing staff, and was well compensated. Cheryl was known to be very empathetic toward her direct reports. But her boss, who was always Cheryl's biggest supporter and a personal friend, began to crack under the pressure of her tremendously increased responsibilities and diminished authority. Cheryl, the only person her boss could trust, somehow became her "whipping girl."

Over a period of just five months, Cheryl's worklife became a living hell, filled with petty humiliations and constant second-guessing by her insecure boss. Her boss would publicly ridicule Cheryl for caring about her employees. To make matters worse, Cheryl's boss began to cut professional corners to "make the numbers." Cheryl sought out professional advice and ended up quitting to save her soul. When she was able to look back on the situation objectively, Cheryl realized that she wasted *way* too much empathy on her boss and was abused for being too empathetic with her employees, whom she was simply trying to protect.

ASSESS YOUR EMPATHY

Take the following assessment to find out how empathetic you are. Each sentence describes a situation which could occur, or which may be similar to a situation that you have actually experienced. Without taking too much time to answer, circle the response that best describes how you would respond—or actually did respond—to the situation.

1. One of your direct reports has been bursting into tears for the last several weeks.
   a. You call her into your office, ask her to sit down and tell you what's bothering her, because you really want to know what's causing her such distress.
   b. You suggest she take a day off this week because she's obviously stressed out.
   c. You ignore her crying and ask her how she's progressing on the department report.

2. You and your boss are not close. She is very buttoned up and structured, and you find her management style, as well as her personal style, difficult to deal with. She has just asked you for some information, but her request seems unreasonable to you. You:
   a. Ask her if you can meet with her because you really want to understand the pressure she's dealing with.
   b. Tell her that you know it's her responsibility to be on top of the information she's asking you to give her, but you can't satisfy her request for a few days.
   c. Tell her that you are very frustrated with her endless requests for information, many of which seem meaningless and a waste of your time.

3. Whenever you read a newspaper story about someone less fortunate than you:
   a. Your first instinct is to find out how you can help. In fact, you are known to provide a "safe harbor" to every person or stray animal that crosses your path.
   b. On occasion, you'll write a check and send it.
   c. Don't feel it's really your social responsibility to help other people.

4. Even when you don't understand someone else's point of view, you try very hard to understand "where they are coming from" before making a decision.

    a. Yes, without exception!

    b. It really depends on the situation and the people involved.

    c. Not usually, because I'm pretty clear about what is right or wrong.

5. When you don't like someone you work with, you believe that the best strategy for dealing with that person is to:

    a. Try to get inside his head and heart and really figure out his motives.

    b. Stand up to him and challenge him when I can.

    c. Avoid him whenever I can, because I'm never going to like him.

6. The most important elements to pay attention to when someone is talking are:

    a. The person's mood, body language, and possible motivations.

    b. What the person is saying, along with his body language.

    c. The content of what the person is saying, along with the words he uses.

7. When you are involved in an emotional situation at work, you:

    a. Concentrate on understanding and isolating your emotions first, before reacting to the other person's emotions.

    b. Ignore your own thoughts and feelings in an attempt to understand the other person's feelings.

    c. Allow yourself to get swept up in the other person's emotional state, even when it's negative.

8. The people closest to you would describe you as:

    a. Someone who really listens well and makes other people feel important or even special.

    b. A person who is pretty consistent in her approach to others.

    c. Someone who is probably more focused on her own agenda or goals, rather than on other people's.

9. You believe that a person in a leadership role should always:

  a. Give his direct reports plenty of encouragement and support to enable them to deliver good results, and maintain a positive attitude even when things go awry.

  b. Concentrate on keeping his department trouble-free and stable, since there are employees who will do a good job and those who won't, regardless of training or feedback.

  c. Prod direct reports to do their jobs right, rewarding or punishing them accordingly. In other words, always let them know who the boss is so they'll do what they are supposed to do.

10. When you are involved in a disagreement with someone at work, you:

  a. Always ask for and try to understand the other person's perspective first.

  b. Sometimes make a decision without considering the other person's opinion because you are confident that you are right, based upon your superior knowledge of the situation.

  c. Usually predetermine the way you will handle a situation regardless of the other person's input.

SCORE KEY

Add the number of times you circled the letter *a* and write the total here: _____
Add the number of times you circled the letter *b* and write the total here: _____
Add the number of times you circled the letter *c* and write the total here: _____
If you circled mostly *a* answers:

  You are extremely empathetic toward other people. Your first tendency is to try to relate to and understand the person's position before thinking about yourself. You usually feel in tune with the people you work with, even if you don't particularly like some of them, or disagree with their approach.

If you circled more *b* answers:

  Your level of empathy depends upon the situation and the people involved. You work at using empathy with others but sometimes let your own feelings and attitude overrule them. When faced with a situation that is emotional or adversarial, first try to pause and focus on what the other person's intentions or motives might be, before considering your own. This will help to defuse the emotion.

If you circled more *c* answers:

You haven't learned to be empathetic toward other people. Try to stop and listen to and understand the opinions and actions of others, especially if they are different from your own. If you have trouble understanding another person's perspective, ask questions and accept the fact that there will always be a different way of looking at things that may be just as valid as yours. Life is like that. Your ability to understand, or even make an effort to understand, other people's feelings will have a profound impact on your success or failure at work—and in life.

If your score indicates that you are short on empathy, the next section of this chapter will give you a chance to understand why and how you can learn to use empathy to benefit yourself and others.

TIPS AND TECHNIQUES FOR IMPROVING YOUR EMPATHY

LEARNING TO RESPOND

To master the art of empathy, you need to learn how to give appropriate responses, both verbal and nonverbal, to the behavioral cues other people send you. To do this, it's important to pay close attention to many things happening on many levels, all at the same time. Read the following list of items along with each definition, and check the items that you *honestly* feel describe your typical behavior in your day-to-day interactions with other people.

Nonverbal Communication

__ Body movement—Leaning in the direction of the person with whom you are interacting.

__ Listening—Actively paying attention to the content, tone, *and intent* of what the person is saying—without interrupting—and giving a thoughtful, sincere, and appropriate reply.

__ Eye contact—Maintaining an interested and unwavering gaze toward the person you are talking to, for the majority of time that you are conversing with them.

__ Smiling—Showing a warm and genuine smile, at the appropriate time and place.

__ Attitude—Conveying a positive mood and a feeling of openness and receptivity toward others.

Verbal Communication

__ Language—Carefully choosing words, phrases, and sentences that demonstrate genuine interest in and attentiveness to the person you are talking to. Instead of saying, "That's happened to me before," say, "Tell me more. I would like to understand what you are going through."

__ Jargon—Using the "language" of the person with whom you are communicating. For example, if you are talking to someone who doesn't work in your industry, avoid using company-specific acronyms.

__ Conversation and "small talk"—Being aware of the importance of "breaking the ice" before moving right into business, demonstrating verbal adeptness, and showing interest and bringing others out.

__ Questioning—Asking clarifying questions that require the person you are asking to give you information and express his or her emotions in the process.

Below are some helpful tips for learning how to improve the items you did not check above.

- **Body movement**—Did you know that actually pointing your heart in the direction of every person you meet can give you a warm and approachable demeanor? How you use your body can convey openness and receptivity to others, or not. Think about it. Do you generally use "open body language" (uncrossed arms and legs, ease in facing someone, good eye contact, smiling, leaning forward, flexible shoulders, and a generally relaxed aura) or the opposite? You may be so accustomed to presenting yourself in a certain way (arms folded across your chest or hands in your pockets) that you may be totally unaware of your tendency to exhibit "closed body language."

- **Listening**—Listening is the key to empathy. We humans spend more of our waking moments listening than just about anything else except breathing. Yet it's been estimated that most people use only about 25 percent of their listening capacity at work. This means that we ignore, distort, forget, or misunderstand 75 percent of what we hear. Listening involves the ability to pay attention not just to words but the underlying intent the person has. It's important to manage "filters"—those things that attach personal meaning to information as it is presented—such as memories, biases, expectations, emotional hot buttons, and your attitude. If, for example, your last conversation with your coworker was unsettling and uncomfortable, it could be easy to let these feelings carry into your next discussion.

The four keys to listening well:
1. Pay attention.
2. Select what's important.
3. Be alert to emotional messages.
4. Ask pertinent questions.

How to Listen Up

- The tone of voice, nonverbal cues, and body language of the person talking to you can affect how well you listen.
- Whether you're talking on the phone or face-to-face, make a conscious effort to focus on what the other person is saying, as well as on their nonverbal cues. Don't let yourself be distracted by a daydream, your computer screen, or TV.
- **Eye contact**—In *How to Connect in Business,* author Nicholas Boothman suggests this easy exercise for maintaining better eye contact: Make a mental note of the eye color of everyone you meet for one day. Doing this will force you to look into someone's eyes every time.
- **Smiling**—Research shows that women smile more often than men do. Whatever your gender, Boothman has a fun suggestion for smil-

ing more often: Put your face close to a mirror, look yourself right in the eyes, and say the word "great" in as many ways as you can. Eventually, you'll start laughing at yourself. Repeat the exercise once a day for three days. Each time you are going to meet someone, say "great" under your breath three times and you'll smile.

- **Attitude**—Many of the Eleven Keys can influence your attitude. For example, your Confidence level, both in yourself and in others, can determine whether your attitude is positively or negatively charged. Curiosity is crucial because the more you learn and understand about a given issue, problem, or situation, the more likely you will be able to alter your attitude about it. Optimism, the natural tendency to expect a good outcome even in the face of adversity, is all about having trust in other people and a generally positive outlook on life. Humor can be a fantastic tool for letting go of stress, frustration, and tension when you are trying to cope with a tough situation. While your attitude can be influenced by superficial factors such as not getting enough sleep or being stuck in traffic, if you make a conscious effort to make a positive shift in your attitude when such everyday annoyances make their appearance (as they often do), you can actually reduce your stress level!

- **Language**—While words are the least significant part of a message in verbal communication, using inappropriate words or phrases can negatively affect your interaction with someone, *especially when you are trying to be empathetic.* In searching for "the right words" to use in a situation where you want to comfort someone who is obviously experiencing emotional pain or distress, it can be helpful to think in terms of language that is "positive" or "active." For example, say, "How can I help you?" instead of "I wish I could help." Or, if the person thanks you, instead of responding, "No problem," say, "It was my pleasure." If you're just not "getting" what the other person is trying to tell you, say, "What else do I need to understand?" instead of, "I'm not sure I understand what you're telling me."

- **Know when to use jargon**—Using "inside words" or language that the person you are talking to does not understand will only serve to dilute your communication. On the other hand, using "slang" words that the person is familiar with can be helpful, but only if you can do so without sounding phony, stilted, or condescending. Choose your words carefully to avoid falling into using expressions or "figures of speech" that are meaningless to the other person.

- **Make conversation**—A key to building trust and creating rapport with others is knowing how to make conversation and use small talk to break the ice and to connect with people you've just met or don't know well or are uncomfortable speaking with about a particular topic. It's also known as *schmoozing*. Even impromptu conversations can turn into meaningful "communication moments." Good conversation is an art, but one that can be learned. A common technique for making conversation is to "plug into" a pattern of organization, such as past-present-future. If a colleague is explaining to you that she feels sad because her son has left for college, you could ask her if she has experienced this with any other children in the past. You can then ask her questions about her son and where he's going to college and, last, ask her if she has any other children who will be entering college in the future. Even if you're talking about a current event such as a playoff game or a bridge collapsing, you can discuss the pros and cons or compare the situation to other situations that are similar. Generally speaking, small talk refers to topics like weather, sports, and immediate current events.

- **Ask questions**—Page 75 in Key #2: Curiosity explains how to ask different types of questions. Clarifying questions are open-ended questions that can begin with words such as "where," "when," "what," "how," and "who." Examples are: "Where did it happen?" "When did it happen?" "What are you referring to?" "How did it happen?" and "Who was involved?" Even when you think you understand what someone is telling you, in order to really empathize, it's important to do more clarifying rather than less.

Unlike some of the other Keys, having too much empathy isn't usually a negative. However, take care not to become a "bleeding heart" who is habitually blinded to reality. Also, if you are empathetic by nature, learn to assess each situation and become self-protective accordingly, lest you run the risk of jeopardizing your emotional or physical well-being in the course of trying to look out for others. Remember what happened to Cheryl, whom you met earlier in this chapter?

If being overly responsive to the feelings of others is a chronic problem for you, stop and do an "emotional temperature check" on yourself. Are you being overly attentive to others in a given situation because you want them to like you or think you are a good person? Are you being realistic? Are you paying enough attention to your own needs and those of the people you care most about? Answering these questions about yourself will put your level of empathy in perspective and also allow you time to think about someone else you should have empathy for—yourself!

CREATE AN ACTION PLAN

Learning to have more empathy for others isn't easy. It takes time and requires that you to stop thinking only about yourself and make a *conscious effort* to focus on other people.

Throughout his career, Bob, a sales executive with a major consulting firm, has gotten feedback that he needs to be more empathetic to his employees, who distrust and are afraid of him. His employer has sent him away to executive "charm school," but as time goes on, Bob reverts to his old "business only" behavior. While it's unlikely that Bob will ever turn into another Mother Teresa, both he and his staff can only benefit from a sincere attempt on Bob's part to change his management style from cold and dictatorial to understanding and human.

The first step is for Bob to come up with an action plan aimed at achieving a few simple goals.

Here is Bob's action plan:

My goal: I am going to work at "putting myself into my employees' shoes" in every situation.

MY SHORT-TERM OBJECTIVES/ACTIVITIES:

1. The next time I talk with each of my eight direct reports, I will start off our discussion by making eye contact with him or her and saying, "How are you doing?" I will really listen to his or her response—even if it's just a polite, one-word answer. Then, after we begin discussing the work issue or problem at hand, before telling him or her what to do, I will ask one of the following questions to understand his or her possible concerns:

   "If you had the choice, what would you most like to happen (or do) now?"

   "Can you tell me three things that concern you about this?"

   "What do you consider to be the primary thing that we should focus on?"

   "What do you think you, or we, should be working to achieve in this situation?"

MY MEDIUM-TERM OBJECTIVES/ACTIVITIES:

1. Confidentially ask Bert to share the techniques he uses with his people. Bert really seems to relate well to his employees and they confide in him.

MY LONG-TERM OBJECTIVE/ACTIVITY:

1. Work on softening my approach. Specifically, the areas I will focus on are:

- Reframing my comments to avoid making judgmental statements that might embarrass my staff or hurt their feelings. For example, when Suzanne was late to my staff meeting last week, I called her "irresponsible" in front of everyone. If Suzanne is late again, I could remark that everyone missed her, ask if she's OK, really listen to her answer, and respond accordingly.

- Stop using demanding or unfeeling language and start being more polite when I ask for something from my staff. I also know that I can be abrupt and forget to say "please" and "thank you."

- Remember to avoid using the word "you" in an accusatory way and substitute the words "we" or "us." Yesterday, I said to Celeste, "You missed another deadline." I could have said, "We really need to meet our deadlines in the future."

Now, it's time to fill out your own action plan. As we discussed earlier in this chapter, developing empathy isn't easy. Where to start? Work on some basic communication skills, like the ones Bob has outlined in his action plan.

My goal:

_____
_____
_____

My short-term objectives/activities:

_____
_____
_____

By when: _____

My medium-term objectives/activities:

_____
_____
_____

By when: _____

My long-term objectives/activities:

_____
_____
_____

By when: _____

Whether or not empathy is an area you need to work on, you're bound to work with people who either don't have enough empathy or have too much—both of which can be bad for business.

In his perennial best-seller, _How to Win Friends and Influence People_, human-relations expert Dale Carnegie lists six simple principles for making other people like you.

All are based on empathy:

1. Become genuinely interested in other people.
2. Smile.
3. Remember that a person's name is to that person the sweetest and most important sound in any language.

4. Be a good listener and encourage others to talk about themselves.
5. Talk in terms of the other person's interests.
6. Make the other person feel important—and do it sincerely.

Some of us are born or raised with a strong capacity for empathy. And then there are the rest of us, who learn to develop empathy later on in life. The ticket to developing empathy is motivation—you must really recognize the value of this subtle but all-important Key and be willing to incorporate it into your personal repertoire of communication skills.

This quote, posted on the Web site advancingwomen.com, says it all: "There is no formula for empathy. It almost never comes as a bolt out of the blue, like being struck by lightning. Almost always it is a determined process of chipping away at those things you do not know or understand about the other person. Like exercising every day, the attempt to understand, relate to, and communicate with others is a process where you slowly build that capacity in yourself, just as you would build a muscle."

Key #5:
Flexibility

This is my way . . .
What is your way?
The way doesn't exist.
—FRIEDRICH NIETZSCHE

Flexibility is a quality of character that allows one to accept change and make suitable adjustments to accommodate it. The word stems from the Latin word *flexere,* which means "to bend."

Peter Suedfeld, professor emeritus of psychology at the University of British Columbia, has spent the last forty years studying the psychology of survival, and his research shows that, "Beyond the fundamental will to survive, the foremost character of a survivor is intellectual flexibility." Typically, he explains, people under extreme stress are more likely to become rigid, which only decreases their chance of survival. "True survivors are extremely adaptable people," notes Dr. Suedfeld. "They know how to improvise. If one solution doesn't work, they try another. They don't fixate on one answer. They keep an open mind, searching for options, developing strategies."

When you think about the metaphors that we all use to describe high-pressure situations at work ("I got hit by an avalanche of e-mails from accounting!" "My staff is drowning in follow-up work from that planning meeting!"), the term "the psychology of survival" makes a lot of sense. You don't need a Ph.D. to understand that a person's ability to cope successfully with constant change in the workplace is directly tied to his or her ability to remain flexible.

Think about it. You are constantly in flux. How many directives have been given to you within the past six months to do new tasks or approach projects differently? How often does your boss, your department, and the company shift priorities? How many times have you had to take a new approach, or behave differently so that you can accommodate the changes? If you're like most people who work, your answers are, "often" and "all the time!"

In the 1980s and 1990s, many larger companies discovered that in order to stay competitive, make money, and meet their shareholders' expectations, they had to be prepared to make quick and, at times, dramatic shifts in the way they did business. They also realized that most of their employees weren't comfortable with rapid change, or equipped to deal with it, either psychologically or from a skills standpoint. Back in those days, bringing in outside consultants and trainers to teach employees how to manage change was a common practice. Now, however, if you are paid to do a job, no matter what your level or whether you've been trained on how to deal with change, *it is expected that you deal with change adeptly and without complaint*. Despite this universal corporate expectation, handling constant change is still difficult for most people. Entrepreneurs and the self-employed aren't spared from the whirlwind of change either.

Change makes most people anxious. Why? Because change usually requires that we:

1. Accept a loss of control over our own destiny.
2. Live with uncertainty and ambiguity.
3. Endure a certain level of discomfort, either physical or psychological or both.

Since we can't always predict what the outcome of a given change will be, we may initially react by jumping to a conclusion—whether logical or illogical—that the change will result in a penalty, not a pay-off. Despite the temporary discomfort that change may impose on us, the ability to remain flexible can be a critical factor in decreasing the anxiety that accompanies it.

When someone becomes too focused on plans, ideas, or procedures that may have existed in the past ("This is the way things are done!"), he will come across to others as rigid. Most people have a hard time dealing with a person who is inflexible, especially at work, where teamwork is often essential to accomplishing goals.

Kay is a well-respected finance professional at her company. But when it comes to collaborating with others to generate ideas or solve problems, Kay's coworkers avoid her. When someone suggests a different way of handling something, she purses her lips and says, "I've worked here for eleven years, and I think I know exactly how we should handle this." After a few such encounters with Kay, most people run the other way. The only people Kay works well with are those who are unassertive, unconfident, or indecisive. Why is Kay like this?

When faced with the need to make a change, most people tend to focus externally when what they really need to do is look at their own attitudes and behaviors and to figure out how they may be contributing to the status quo that needs changing. In other words, they need to be flexible. According to the *Successful Manager's Handbook,* someone's ability to be flexible is driven by three things: the way she thinks, her assumptions and filters (personal biases, beliefs, memories, "hot buttons," etc.), and her emotional state. To deal appropriately and effectively with change, all her thoughts, beliefs, and feelings must be aligned with the change. When they aren't, she demonstrates inflexibility, which will be frustrating for everyone who has to work with her.

Here's an example: Stu works in sales. Recently, his manager approached Stu and told him that his boss had asked that he rearrange the client territory by size of accounts. The biggest accounts will go to the most senior salesperson, the next largest accounts to the next salesperson by seniority, and so on. Since six of the other eight salespeople on the team have been with the company longer than Stu, his immediate reaction to the news was to feel angry and slighted.

Stu's last employer, a competitor of his present company's, had re-organized in the same way, and it was a disaster. In fact, it was a big reason that Stu left his last job. So, upon hearing the news, instead of taking it in and allowing himself time to walk away calmly, cool down, and think through how the restructuring could work for his customers, the organization, and himself, Stu gave in to his angry emotions. He made an angry comment and stormed out of his boss's office. For weeks afterward, Stu refused to talk to his boss. He allowed his anger to rule his behavior instead of presenting positive ideas to his boss about how he would work with him to make the change work. In the end, Stu's rigid behavior hurt him because it did serious damage to his relationship with his boss.

Flexibility is more than just a coping mechanism for change. It's a crucial element of creativity and innovation, problem solving, decision-making, and relationship building. Flexible people see change as an opportunity rather than as a threat. They are risk-takers.

Of the Eleven Keys, Flexibility is one of the easiest to spot. The flexible individual listens receptively to new ideas or suggested approaches, doesn't get upset when plans change, shows respect to those in positions of authority when new policies or priorities are introduced, and looks for the positive side of proposed changes. A flexible person is empathetic toward others, showing a readiness to try to understand ideas or values that may be different from his or her own.

The body language of a flexible person is typically "open," with relaxed movements, steady eye contact, and a smile. In fact, flexible people always seem to have more fun and are more pleasant to be around.

An inflexible person presents quite a different picture. This individual tends to complain or to become easily upset about a sudden change in plans or a new way of doing things. His or her natural tendency is to cling to the old ways without presenting a solid rationale for maintaining the status quo. Because he or she is so quick to respond negatively to new information, the inflexible individual has little time to do active listening and tends to focus more on his or her own needs than on those of colleagues or of the organization as a whole. Sometimes the very idea of change can seem so threatening to this individual that his or her first response is to simply shut down. The rigid attitude of the inflexible person may be reflected in "closed" body language, such as crossed arms, pinched or pursed lips, darting eyes, frowning, and hunched posture. Inflexible people tend to be judgmental and uptight. In the absence of other redeeming personal traits, their negativity can be a turnoff to others.

RELATED KEYS 🔑━━

KEY #5: FLEXIBILITY

🔑 **Curiosity** tops the list. If you are driven by a desire to learn and understand what you don't already know, your motivation will outweigh your tendency to remain in your usual "comfort zone" of thinking and behaving.

🔑 **Optimism** enables you to see the potentially positive side of change. No matter what the actual outcome, your belief that things will ultimately turn out OK will help you to get through the transition and land on your feet.

🔑 **Empathy** gives you the ability to see the situation from another person's point of view. When change comes from the top, your ability to put yourself in the other person's shoes can help you understand the reasons for the change, even if you don't agree with it.

🔑 **Humor** acts as a lens that allows you to step back and see the situation more objectively and put it into proper perspective. Change usually makes most people nervous at first; humor can take the edge off and aid in the transition process.

🔑 **Self-awareness,** when it's balanced, enables you to take a look at yourself when you're feeling inflexible and make an adjustment in your attitude and behavior.

POINTERS FOR WORKING WITH PEOPLE WHO LACK FLEXIBILITY OR ARE OVERLY FLEXIBLE

Someone consistently says no or tries to shut you down, refusing to try an alternate approach to a challenging issue, decision, or problem.

If you are a peer: Document each time he has tried to shut you down. Next, schedule a one-on-one meeting with him for the sole purpose of discussing how his behavior makes you feel. Tell him you're very interested in collaborating with him to achieve your mutual business goals, but that you find it difficult to do so when he automatically closes up. If he argues with you or pretends he doesn't know what you're talking about, pull out your notes and replay the situations that have occurred. Be very careful not to criticize him personally, but instead address his behavior and how it has affected you.

If you are his manager: Set expectations and goals with him, then give him constructive feedback about his inflexible behavior and point out how it interferes with business (documentation is a must here). Offer to coach him to help him overcome his inflexible tendencies.

If you are less senior: Be wary of arguing with an inflexible senior manager. Instead, compliment him on his opinions, expertise, or perspective. Next, ask him if you can run some new ideas by him in the near future. An inflexible person is very interested in being in control of a situation so it's imperative not to make him feel as if his control is slipping. Keep persisting at approaching him with new ideas or ways of doing things so that eventually he may become more flexible. Obviously, there's no guarantee that he will, but it's worth trying.

Someone always seems more concerned with proving that she is "right" than in collaborating with others to find a constructive resolution to the problem at hand.

If you are a peer: Assure your stubborn coworker that you value her experience and other strengths that she brings to the table. Tell her that although she may not be aware of it, every encounter you have with her feels like a competition. Ask her to remember that you're on the same team, that you share a desired outcome, and that you're much more likely to achieve it as colleagues rather than as competitors.

If you are her manager: Sit her down and try to understand what it is that is threatening her. Explain to her that her obstinate behavior is disrupting productivity and that her coworkers are apprehensive about working with her because of her counterproductive behavior. Assure her that you recognize that her challenging behavior means she's passionate about her work, but that a better approach would be to say yes once in a while.

If you are less senior: Set up a meeting with her. Take a deep breath and tell her that it's not easy to tell her this, but that she is seen as a role model and people are confused by her seemingly adversarial approach to working together. It's always risky to give tough feedback to someone who is senior to you, so you'll have to weigh whether or not the possible consequences are worth it. Perhaps you can take a gently joking posture with her, depending upon whether she has a sense of humor.

Someone is consistently fearful of trying new experiences, preferring to retreat or hide, and do things the same way she has always done them.

If you are a peer: Praise her for her real strengths and tell her that you value her as a person and as a coworker, and that you really need her participation and contributions to help you do your job or to achieve your mutual business goals. Offer to be her peer coach or suggest a person that she admires to coach her to help her overcome her fear of risk taking.

If you are her manager: Tell her how much you value her talent and contributions. Explain that the organization also values risk-takers and employees who are constantly thinking of ways to make improvements. Offer to sit down with her to create a simple development plan to help her learn to take new approaches and have new experiences.

If you are less senior: If you want her to take a new approach in doing something, be sure you have researched as much as you can and laid out the implications of using the new method. This includes the favorable business results that will occur when she takes the new approach. If she sees that taking a different approach will really help her reach the team's goals, maybe she'll try it.

Someone never expresses an opinion and seems always willing to go along with the majority vote, either because he has a strong need to avoid "rocking the boat" or, deep down, he's inflexible.

If you are a peer: Show friendly interest and insist on hearing his opinion because you value what he thinks. Try this approach in a one-on-one meeting first, to gain your coworker's trust and help to increase his comfort level. Then, in a kind, lighthearted, nonthreatening manner, try it in a group meeting. If he still has trouble responding, let him off the hook. Be patient; don't give up. You may need to repeat this approach over a period of time to help your colleague gradually out of his shell. When he makes an effort, even a small one, be sure to respond with respectful praise.

If you are his manager: Unfortunately, it is difficult to read someone who never expresses an opinion, and it's unlikely that your colleagues have a read on your direct report either. Ask your employee what his opinion is outright—and if he waffles or cops out of a real answer, ask him what is inhibiting him from expressing his opinions and explain to him that it is an expectation that he contribute by speaking up, not just by doing his job.

If you are less senior: Make an effort to ask him for his opinion or for feedback as often as you can so that you can understand his perspective. When he does tell you what he thinks, be sure to listen and comment thoughtfully. Perhaps if you gain his trust by listening to his viewpoint and soliciting his opinions, you can develop a more productive relationship and more acceptance from him for doing things differently if he's resisted in the past.

Your typical reactions to requests, new directives, and other changes at work, as well as the feedback you receive from coworkers, will give you clues as to how flexible you are. Just as with the other Eleven Keys, not being flexible enough or being too flexible can work against you on the job; balance is the ideal to strive for. If flexibility is not your strong point at work, it may be time for you to learn to loosen up. If, on the other hand, your inclination is to be too flexible, you may be giving your coworkers the message that you lack interest, motivation, or confidence. Your behavior may make it hard for them to take you seriously or to not dismiss you as a pushover. Learning to listen to your own instincts, voice your opinions, and stand up for your convictions can make you a more effective and desirable member of any team.

ASSESS YOUR FLEXIBILITY

Take the following assessment to help you decide just how well you adapt to change or unexpected circumstances. Indicate the degree to which you agree with each statement by circling the response that best describes you.

1. I usually react to suggestions or advice first, before thinking through the consequences.
   Almost always   Sometimes   Rarely

2. I believe that I know what the right approach is to getting something done, even if I haven't done it often before.
   Almost always   Sometimes   Rarely

3. I don't really feel comfortable receiving unsolicited advice from colleagues about how to do things.
   Almost always   Sometimes   Rarely

4. I follow a pretty specific routine at work that seems to work well for me.
   Almost always   Sometimes   Rarely

5. I don't see the point of constantly seeking out new ways to solve problems and improve business, since everything changes so fast anyway.

    Almost always   Sometimes   Rarely

6. When I'm faced with major change, it takes a long time for me to accept it, deal with it, and bounce back.

    Almost always   Sometimes   Rarely

7. I really believe that I'm a flexible person; it's just that I like to feel comfortable with knowing what's going to happen before I try something new.

    Almost always   Sometimes   Rarely

8. I believe that there are still plenty of companies that value loyal employees who desire stability and who want to continue doing the same kind of work over a long period of time.

    Almost always   Sometimes   Rarely

9. Routines, consistency, and my regular habits are very important to me; I don't like disrupting these if I don't have to.

    Almost always   Sometimes   Rarely

10. Once I've made up my mind about something, I like to stick with my choice, because I know that I make solid decisions based upon sound judgment.

    Almost always   Sometimes   Rarely

11. Planning, research, and analysis are the most important aspects of working smart, so I believe that once a decision has been made based upon these things, it's very important to stick with it.

    Almost always   Sometimes   Rarely

SCORE KEY

Add the number of times you circled the answer "Almost always" and multiply this number by 2. Write your score here: _____.

Add the number of times you circled the answer "Sometimes" and multiply this number by 4. Write your score here: _____.

Add the number of times you circled the answer "Rarely" and multiply this number by 6. Write your score here: _____.

Now, add all three numbers for your total score: _____.

52 to 66—You are very flexible. Your ability to switch gears at "the drop of a hat" is impressive and is usually very comfortable for you. You have accepted the constantly changing nature of business and the world at large, and you're typically willing to modify your plans, actions, or attitude to meet the needs of others. Be wary, though, of being *too* flexible. You may be perceived as apathetic, a pushover or people-pleaser, or timid about expressing your ideas and opinions.

37 to 51—You move between being very flexible and getting a bit stuck in your habitual ways of approaching things, ways that may not be appropriate or most effective for the situation at hand. It may be that you are more flexible in one part of your life than another. During the times when your urge is to shut down and take a familiar approach or resist new ideas, try to pause and remember to "go with the flow." Despite feeling some discomfort, you'll manage to balance your flexibility pretty well.

22 to 36—Your chronically rigid behavior often tends to get you into trouble at work because it strains your relationships with coworkers and clients. If you're young, you may be perceived as difficult and opinionated. If you're a little older, you may be viewed as someone who is "set in your ways" and unable to change. In general, an inflexible attitude can become an ingrained personality trait that becomes harder to change as you grow older. Whether you are inflexible because you dislike change, or because your confidence is shaken when you're forced to take a different tack, it's time to work on increasing your flexibility.

Now that you've done some self-exploration, do you know which category you fall into? Are you inflexible? Or do you vacillate between "going with the flow" and staying stuck? If either description fits you, go to the next section of this chapter for practical advice on how to loosen up and "roll with the punches."

Learn to Loosen Up!
What Are You Inflexible About?

It's human nature to stick with what's familiar and comfortable. But constantly closing yourself off from new experiences and possibilities can make you become rigid and boring. Over time, if you insist on staying stuck in your ways, rigidity can become a permanent part of your personality and you will miss out on opportunities to enjoy and enrich your life. This assessment will help you to hone in on some of the things in your life that you've chosen to resist. Without spending too much time on your responses, complete the statements for each category.

Food

I don't like the way _____ tastes or looks.

I have always disliked _____.

I can't understand why anyone would eat _____.

Sports

The only sports I like to watch on television are _____.

The only types of sports I will participate in are _____.

I don't watch or play sports because _____.

Music

I don't like the following types of music: (check your choices)

_____ Rock and roll	_____ Hip-hop
_____ Reggae	_____ Classical
_____ Rap	_____ Pop
_____ Blues	_____ Jazz
_____ Country	_____ Swing

Traveling

I have no interest in traveling to the following places:

1. _____

2. _____

3. _____

4. _____

5. _____

Interests and Activities

I am not interested in trying the following activities (check your choices). If you've already tried it and don't want to do it again, check it anyway.

_____ Hot-air ballooning   _____ Wine tasting

_____ Polo   _____ Knitting

_____ Archery   _____ Horseback riding

_____ Riding a motorcycle   _____ Hiking

_____ Mountain climbing   _____ Take a parachute jump

_____ Scuba diving   _____ Learn to drive a tractor

_____ Fire-walking   _____ Milk a cow

_____ Go on a safari   _____ Take violin lessons

_____ Write an article for your local newspaper   _____ Play chess

_____ Learn about Buddhism   _____ Deep-sea fishing

Taking a Different Approach

Here is a list of common activities and tasks that you may do regularly. Check each activity that you would consider doing differently from the way you are used to doing it.

_____ Cleaning your house   _____ Cooking a meal

_____ Commuting to work   _____ Meeting with your boss

_____ Planning a project at work   _____ Teaching a child something

_____ Handling a conflict or confrontation   _____ Learning a software program

_____ Getting dressed for work   _____ Making a major purchase

_____ Taking a trip

This assessment is designed to allow you to see, on paper, how you may exhibit inflexibility, whether knowingly or unknowingly. Next, go back and look at your answers in each category, and answer the questions below for each section.

But first, take a look at Kerry's responses below so that you can use them as an example when you assess your lack of flexibility with your responses.

KERRY'S RESPONSES:

Food

I don't like the way beets taste. Why? Because my mother used to make me eat beets several times a week when I was young. I haven't tasted a beet in twenty years.

I dislike cottage cheese. I don't like foods with mushy textures.

I can't understand why anyone would eat anything that's alive. It makes me feel like vomiting to think of eating something that isn't dead!

Sports

The only sports I like to watch on television are golf, tennis, and figure skating. Most team sports bore me.

The only types of sports I will participate in are volleyball, skiing, and softball. Why? Because I'm not a good athlete.

I don't watch or play sports because I am uncoordinated. I was always the last person to be picked for sports teams as a child.

Music

I don't like the following types of music: (check your choices)

_____ Rock and roll   _____ Hip-hop

_____ Reggae   _____ Classical

_____ Rap   _____ Pop

_____ Blues   _____ Jazz

_✓_ Country   _____ Swing

Why did you choose the types of music you did? I checked "Country" because I find it depressing. Come to think of it, I haven't heard any new country artists in many years.

Traveling

I have no interest in traveling to the following places:

1. India—too populated and very poor.
2. Israel—the conflict scares me.
3. Idaho—a cultural wasteland.
4. China—I wouldn't like the food and it's so far away.
5. Outer space—Simply no interest, I never thought about why.

Interests and Activities

I am not interested in trying the following activities:

_____ Hot-air ballooning   _____ Wine tasting

_____ Playing polo   _✓_ Knitting

_✓_ Practicing archery   _✓_ Horseback riding

_____ Riding a motorcycle   _____ Hiking

____✓____ Mountain climbing   _____ Taking a parachute jump

____✓____ Scuba diving   _____ Learning to drive a tractor

____✓____ Fire-walking   ____✓____ Milking a cow

____✓____ Going on a safari   _____ Taking violin lessons

_____ Writing an article for your local newspaper   _____ Playing chess

_____ Learning about Buddhism   _____ Deep-sea fishing

Why did I choose the things I did?

Practicing archery—Seems like a dumb sport.
Knitting—I don't have too much patience for sitting for long periods of time.
Horseback riding—My ex-boyfriend rode horses, and whenever I see a horse, I think of him. It's not a good memory.
Mountain climbing—I'm not exactly the great-outdoors type.
Scuba diving—I really like most water sports but wear contacts so wouldn't have fun because I couldn't see.
Fire-walking—Why in the world would I want to do this?
Milking a cow—I grew up in the Midwest and have already milked cows.
Going on a safari—too many bugs and reptiles for me.

Notice that many of Kerry's answers were based on her past experiences and that, in many cases, it's been a long time since she's had those experiences. For example, she has totally dismissed the idea of playing sports because she remembers how she felt when she was twelve years old and the last one chosen by her schoolmates for teams. At thirty-six, Kerry is allowing a twenty-four-year-old memory to rule her preferences about how she wants to spend her leisure time. Some of Kerry's other choices are based on negative assumptions, such as not wanting to visit China because she's sure that she wouldn't like the food. Kerry has rejected the idea of doing and exploring other activities that she really knows nothing about. For example, her negative take on archery.

Kerry's responses show that risk taking, an important part of flexibility, does not come naturally to her.

Now it's your turn. Think about the reasons for the answers you gave on your assessment.

Why did you choose the food you chose?

_____

_____

_____

Why did you select the sports you did?

_____

_____

_____

Why did you choose the music you did?

_____

_____

_____

Why did you write down the geographic locations you did?

_____

_____

_____

Why did you identify the activities you did?

_____

_____

_____

Why did you choose some routine tasks and not others?

_____

_____

_____

This exercise was designed to help you see how automatic your rigid responses can be. Kerry was shocked to discover her obvious tendency toward inflexible behavior. While she has often been told by family and friends that she needs to open up and try new things, she honestly thought that she had been doing that until she answered these questions. Was this your experience, too? If so, then it's time to think about how you can start to become more flexible in your relationships. As you've learned elsewhere in this book, the way in which we communicate with others, both verbally and nonverbally, has a lot to do with how we are perceived. This next assessment can help you identify some changes you can make to put some elasticity in your communication style, especially at work.

TIPS AND TECHNIQUES FOR IMPROVING YOUR FLEXIBILITY

Flex It! Change Your Communication Style and Improve Your Relationships

The following assessment highlights six important areas where "bending and stretching" your "flexibility muscles" can work wonders in your relationships! Each of the six areas represents a characteristic of a flexible person.

- **The ability to respond in a sensitive, thoughtful manner to people in difficult circumstances.** Wilhelm works for Fred whose boss, Declan, just resigned from the company. Instead of worrying about how Wilhelm's job will be affected, he immediately called Fred to ask him if he was OK and if there was anything he could do to help him during the transition.

  Now, think of an unexpected, difficult situation that recently occurred in your workplace. Did you focus immediately on yourself and how you were affected? Or, did you do what Wilhelm did and focus your attention on being supportive of the other people involved?

  _____

  _____

- **The ability to adjust quickly to a change of plans.** Adapting to change with a positive attitude, such as taking a different approach to a project, regardless of how long you've spent on planning to implement it in a certain way, is an important quality. Dirk is a product manager for a consumer package-goods company. He's responsible for half a dozen products at a time and spends six months planning their rollout. Every year, his company decides not to launch two or three products. Dirk knows that this is a given, so he's learned to allow himself a day to recover psychologically from the letdown he feels each time a product he has worked on is pulled. This clever way of planning for his own emotional well-being enables Dirk to move on with relatively little stress.

  Now, think of an important plan you've made that has changed unexpectedly because of circumstances beyond your control. How did you react outwardly? How long did it take for you to recover internally (emotionally)? Looking back, how could you have handled your reaction to the situation differently?

  _____

  _____

- **Being able to align with others' needs and perspectives.** Making a sincere effort to understand and be supportive of other people, even when you don't always agree with their views, for the purpose of maintaining a healthy relationship. Franco finds it difficult to agree with anything his coworker Pierre does. But long ago, Franco learned that it would benefit him to listen to Pierre's opinionated views and, whenever possible, to look for opportunities to be supportive. As a result, Franco is the only person Pierre trusts at work. Franco's willingness to bend has made their working relationship much easier.

  Think of someone at work with whom you've had trouble getting along. Who is this person? What do you find difficult about them? Try putting yourself in this person's shoes. What are some reasons that might account for their problem behavior? What can _you_ do in the future to make your relationship work better?

  _____

  _____

- **Focusing on priorities outside your own.** Being clear about the priorities of your organization, your boss, and your stakeholders. If you ignore these and focus exclusively on your own personal needs and desires, which may not match those of your workplace "significant others" or of the organization as a whole, you will be viewed as inflexible.

   Frances sets up regular meetings with her boss, her boss's boss, and six other people who impact her job, just to be sure that the work she's doing is in line with their projects and initiatives. As a result, she is always privy to inside information before anyone else in her department, and it always appears to her colleagues that she is placing their needs and interests above her own.

   What about you? Do you tend to decide which aspects of your job are important without taking into consideration other people's priorities? Have you considered planning discussions with your colleagues, on a regular basis, to ascertain whether or not you're putting the appropriate amount of time and energy into the "right" priorities?

   _____

   _____

- **Being open to learning new information and skills.** Being receptive to new ideas that can improve your job, function, department, and organization can keep your mind active and engaged and make work interesting for yourself and your coworkers.

   Phyllis is a first-shift, first-line supervisor for a manufacturing company. She started as a part-time hourly employee and has been promoted four times in five years. Why? Because Phyllis reads business books about concepts such as "lean manufacturing" and "Six Sigma" (a methodology used to measure quality improvement) and then teaches her direct reports the best aspects of these approaches so that the manufacturing process always gets better.

   When was the last time you took the initiative to learn something new that could improve the quality of your work? Are you first in line for learning new practices or training that your organization rolls out? Or do you cower in your cubicle, hoping that no one will notice that you aren't in the front row of the conference room?

Think about something you had to learn recently. How did you approach it?

_____

_____

_____

ARE YOU TOO FLEXIBLE?

If you "go with the flow" no matter what, even if it means compromising your true feelings or convictions, it's likely that your colleagues find you easy to deal with because they never get any argument from you. But there could be a downside for you. Your perpetually easygoing attitude could be giving people the impression that you are chronically indecisive, unassertive, or apathetic to what's going on around you. Even if people like you, and you're skilled at your job, you may be losing out on gaining the respect of your coworkers—an important element of any productive work relationships. Indecisive people (see Key #3: Decisiveness) and people who project low self-confidence (see Key #1: Confidence) tend to go along with the majority opinion because they're afraid of "making waves." Their safety-seeking behavior may make them comfortable, but it fails to inspire respect. Similarly, if you are or even seem to be chronically apathetic, your attitude is probably making it difficult for other people to connect with you emotionally. Even if you don't particularly care about certain issues on the job, it's a good idea to express an opinion now and then, even if your opinion goes against the grain. Letting other people know that you care and are willing to take a stand and show them what you stand for can change their perception of you.

Think about the last two or three situations that you've been asked to become involved in at work that required a decision. Write them on the lines below.

_____

_____

_____

Next, ask yourself these questions:

What was the situation, and what decision was required?

_____

_____

_____

Who asked you for your input? How did you feel about it?

_____

_____

How did you react? Could your reaction be evaluated as overly flexible? If so, why did you behave this way?

_____

_____

CREATE AN ACTION PLAN

If you are inflexible, it's likely that you demonstrate this quality in many aspects of your life. Are you ready to make a change? Focusing on the inflexible behavior that most affects your relationships with other people is a good place to start. Are you like Kay, the financial professional described earlier in this chapter? Kay's coworkers try to avoid working with her on any project that requires her input because it's guaranteed that Kay will shut down before listening to other people's ideas. Inflexibility is especially tough to overcome, so starting small is a good idea. Let's look at Gretchen's action plan.

Gretchen cites her fear of change as the reason for her rigid behavior. Since the company she works for was bought by another firm six months ago, her job as an account manager has changed quite a bit. She receives requests for information from clients and coworkers from all around the United States now and is aware that, quite often, she responds to them in an uptight, negative tone of voice and purposely takes her time getting them the information they've called to request. Recently, Gretchen's boss received some complaints about her attitude and phone manner, and shared them with her. Gretchen admits that the time has come for her to take a good look at her behavior and try to make some changes.

My goal: I am going to react positively and make an effort to be as flexible as possible with everyone at work who contacts me for help.

MY SHORT-TERM OBJECTIVES/ACTIVITIES:

1. The next person to contact me today is going to have a pleasant surprise! I am going to drop everything, no matter what I'm doing, and get the information he or she needs immediately.

2. I am going online to order two books my sister recommended to me on how to deal with change.

MY MEDIUM-TERM OBJECTIVE/ACTIVITY:

1. I am going to research communication courses and sign up for one to take in the next two months. I think that learning some positive communication techniques might help me to do my job better, and might even help me meet men!

MY LONG-TERM OBJECTIVE/ACTIVITY:

1. I am going to ask my human resources department for a 360-degree review (a peer evaluation process) so that I can understand how others perceive me. My friend Marty told me that part of the process is getting help from an executive coach who works with you to create a development plan. This could help me improve in the areas people have identified as being weak spots for me. (I'm sure my unyielding behavior will be one.)

Now, create your own action plan. If you have trouble, think about someone you know whom you view as inflexible. What are some things you'd recommend to help him loosen up?

My goal:

_____

_____

My short-term objectives/activities:

_____

_____

_____

By when: _____

My medium-term objectives/activities:

_____

_____

_____

By when: _____

My long-term objectives/activities:

_____

_____

_____

By when: _____

In today's workplace, knowing how to ebb and flow with change is an *essential* survival skill. People who are truly flexible don't just roll over and go along with anything, but instead listen well to others before reacting or making a decision. They visualize multiple approaches to solving a problem and easily drop the ones that aren't viable. Remember: *A flexible person sees change as an opportunity rather than as a threat.* If flexibility isn't your natural forte, learn to observe people who are flexible and emulate their attitudes and behaviors.

Flexibility is a Key that needs to be fine-tuned during one's entire life. Being flexible isn't always painless or comfortable at first, but remember that change is inevitable and in the long run it guarantees you an easier adjustment to changing circumstances and can help you enrich your relationships, both at work and at home. Author of *On the Job,* Stephen Viscusi, sums it up well: "Flexibility and spontaneous response, not adherence to a preconceived five-year plan, are the very qualities you need if you want to field the situations life tosses you."

Key #6:
Humor

Humor is something that thrives between man's aspirations and his limitations. There is more logic in humor than in anything else. Because, you see, humor is truth.

—VICTOR BORGE

Humor is the capacity to perceive, appreciate, or express what is funny, amusing, incongruous, ludicrous, or absurd about yourself or life's situations. It's a healthy way of putting distance between yourself and a problem in order to put it into perspective.

Humor is always highly personal, individual, and subjective. Someone who finds John Cleese or Chris Rock hysterically funny may be turned off by Rodney Dangerfield or Joan Rivers. A die-hard fan of Lucille Ball's slapstick comedy may not be partial to Jerry Seinfeld's or Whoopi Goldberg's more cerebral style. Regardless of what brand of humor appeals to you, the ability to find humor in stressful or uncomfortable situations—especially at work—can provide important benefits to your psychological and physical well-being.

Humor can defuse negative emotions such as anger and guilt, spark enthusiasm, and inspire motivation. People who use humor as a communication tool tend to have an easier time coping with problems than those who rarely crack a smile. Expressing humor can reduce the inhibitions and increase the self-confidence of individuals who are otherwise shy and introverted by nature. A healthy sense of humor is often the sign of a nimble, intelligent, creative mind.

Jim Chambers, president of Cadbury Schweppes Americas Confectionery, has earned a reputation for using humor to lower employees' inhibitions, connect people at meetings, and help stimulate their thinking. A specific incident stands out in Jim's mind that has always helped him stay on the lighter side of things at work. Years ago, he worked for Nabisco, and one day he raced into his boss's office to give her what he thought was "an amazingly important piece of financial information." She leaned over, took it from Jim's hand, and drawled, "We're not curing cancer—we sell cookies and crackers." What was her point? Whenever someone gets too serious about work, he or she should use humor to put things in perspective.

John Morreall, president of Humorworks, believes, "Anybody who has normal mental development can engage in and benefit from humor. All they have to do is put themselves in a more playful state of mind, giving themselves permission to do something they did very easily when they were three years old."

Laughter, the natural physical reaction to humor, is a universal human response. Laughing can improve both your immune and cardiovascular systems. It can relieve stress and discharge physical and emotional tension. Morreall explains, "When we're stressed, we often feel like we have no control of the situation. We feel helpless. But when we laugh, at least in our minds, we assume some control. We feel able to handle it."

Humor guru William Fry, professor emeritus of psychiatry at Stanford University, found that by the time a child reaches kindergarten, he or she laughs an average of three hundred times a day. Compare this to a study by Rod Martin, professor at the University of Western Ontario, who found that the typical adult laughs only seventeen times a day, and that men and women laugh equally as often, but at different things.

What accounts for this progressive sobering state of affairs? For one thing, managers who are fearful about their own job security tend to think that if people are laughing, they aren't working. Other causes for less humor in the workplace are technology, the fear of being sued for inappropriate behavior such as sexual harassment, and the general stress created by too much work. Once upon a time, it was common for people to tell jokes to each other at work as a way of easing tension and making the workday seem to go faster. Then, e-mail became the communication du jour, and long, written jokes and funny JPEGs were distributed via attachment to large groups of people at the same company and beyond. These days spam, viruses, worms, and stricter monitoring of e-mail have nearly wiped out even this method of sharing a good laugh with one's coworkers.

It seems obvious that most people would prefer to work in a light-hearted, fun environment rather than in a grim, humorless one. Studies have shown that dissatisfied workers tend to be late or absent more often and have poorer attitudes than their happier counterparts. Employees who are satisfied with their work environment tend to be more committed to their jobs and organization, more likely to collaborate with their colleagues, and less likely to leave their jobs. Creativity is higher and customers are happier when the people servicing them are having fun. When someone has to work side by side with a colleague who lacks humor, this can create a very uncomfortable atmosphere because there is no outlet for decreasing stress or creating rapport.

In the short-lived dot-com era, fun environments were the norm. As soon as the economy's bottom dropped around 2000, sober and serious ruled once again. If humor is better, then why aren't more companies focused on creating a fun work environment for their employees?

Alison, a senior finance executive who often uses humor at work, believes the reason for this is because humor is generally misunderstood in the workplace. She has found, from personal experience, that it's easy for the individual who is funny to be perceived as flippant or uncommitted to company goals. Alison has also discovered that peers and bosses can be jealous and resentful of a person such as herself, who is both humorous and successful in business. Since Alison and people like her also tend to be popular socially, they may be viewed as a "triple threat" by colleagues who are insecure and competitive.

Teachers, health-care practitioners, and emergency workers use humor to cope with job-related stress, relieve tension, and gain perspective. Humor can be used in the workplace to serve several purposes: to entertain, to be playful, and to develop relationships, express feelings, or reveal something about ourselves that we may otherwise be uncomfortable talking about. It can also be used to demean others or "put them in their place."

People who use humor for the first two reasons stated above are usually perceived by others as socially attractive and effective communicators. Why? Because using humor appropriately and well is a difficult and complex skill that requires intelligence, creativity, and sensitivity. People with a highly developed sense of humor tend to be successful because they are flexible and able to adapt to a variety of situations and individuals.

HUMOR IN THE WORKPLACE—
WHEN DOES IT STOP BEING FUNNY?

When a person demeans or picks on a coworker, this is not humor—it's sarcasm or, in more extreme cases, verbal abuse. A person who constantly jokes, clowns around, or pulls pranks at work, regardless of the situation, is likely to be perceived by colleagues as someone who doesn't take him- or herself, or the job, seriously enough. Corporate executive Edward Toupin offers some good advice: "If your boss asks you if you have a sense of humor, he's not asking if you're a clown. What he is asking is whether or not you can accept criticism, deal with difficult people, and gracefully handle mistakes without snapping people's heads off when things get stressful." Why? Because using humor as a tension-breaking device is probably the best coping mechanism of all.

RELATED KEYS 🔑━━

KEY #6: HUMOR

🔑━ **Confidence.** Humor involves risk taking as well as a healthy belief in your own ability to get others to identify with your assessment of what is funny.

🔑━ **Curiosity.** The ability to ask questions and to keenly observe human (and animal) behavior in the world at large is the basis of all great humor.

🔑━ **Empathy.** Being able to walk in someone else's shoes can help you make your humor a tool to illuminate or entertain, rather than a weapon to punish or hurt.

🔑━ **Flexibility.** Humorous people tend to be adaptable to diverse people and situations; they often use Humor to adjust to unexpected or unfamiliar circumstances.

🔑━ **Optimism.** While many comedians could be considered pessimists (Jerry Seinfeld, Woody Allen), it's probably easier to be funny if you approach life and its problems from a positive standpoint.

🔑━ **Self-awareness.** Using Humor requires a real awareness of your feelings, thoughts, and emotions.

POINTERS FOR WORKING WITH PEOPLE WHO LACK HUMOR

It's especially frustrating to interact with people who are humorless when you have a well-developed sense of humor. It's almost as if you are speaking another language. And the lack of humor can often drain the creative energy out of a meeting or a project. It can also be difficult when a person has a completely different kind of humor than your own or uses humor to victimize his colleagues.

A coworker takes himself or his work too seriously, all the time.

If you are a peer: Smile at him and try to get him to talk a bit about his personal life, the weather, or other interests he may have. Tell him about a funny movie or TV show you saw recently and ask if he's seen it. Ask what makes him laugh and what kind of humor he likes. Depending upon how important it is that you work more comfortably with this person, ask him to lunch and see whether he reveals a lighter side.

If you are his manager: Tease him gently and make jokes about work-related things, especially when things go wrong. Set an example for being lighthearted and approaching the challenges at work with a smile and a laugh. When he is being very serious, ask him to step back and try to see the humor in the situation.

If you are less senior: If you are a happy person who smiles and laughs, don't change your persona around this person. Be yourself and perhaps your levity will rub off on your higher-up. At the same time, be sure that he doesn't perceive your humorous nature as frivolous. It's important that he realizes that while you are lighthearted, you do take your work seriously—to achieve this, wisely choose when and where to have fun.

A colleague treats you poorly because she seems to be envious of your popularity, which may be a result of your ability to make others laugh.

If you are a peer: Make a special effort to work on your relationship with this person. Joke with her and include her in your work and projects. In other words, make her your friend. Hopefully, she'll come around and feel less threatened. If not, you'll know that you've tried your best to develop a relationship with her.

If you are her manager: Show appreciation for her as an employee and give her recognition as often as is appropriate. Try to learn what her brand of humor is and adjust yours to hers. For example, if she uses sarcastic humor, use the same with her.

If you are less senior: If she is your boss, you should work hard at complementing her skills with yours, being a trustworthy employee, and doing the best possible job. If this isn't enough for your boss to appreciate you and stop being jealous, there's not much else you really can do except be friendly and try to include her in your jokes as often as possible or seems appropriate.

Someone uses humor to take advantage of others or to inflict cruelty, or is generally clueless about how his unkind ribbing adversely affects those who are its target.

If you are a peer: Pull him aside and ask if he has any idea how seriously he affects the morale, confidence, or feelings of the person who is the target of his ribbing. If he pretends naivety, repeat a specific incident and ask him how he would feel if this type of "humor" was directed at him. It's likely that the victim of his unkind humor won't have the courage or confidence to defend him- or herself. Every time the aggressive individual displays the offending behavior, remind him of the impact. If the situation gets out of hand, encourage the victim to file a complaint with human resources, or to consult the company's legal department or an outside labor attorney.

If you are his manager: Sit him down and point out how his cruelty is affecting everyone around him, not just his victim. Ask him to think about how he would feel if he were the person being ridiculed. If he persists in his behavior, tell him that you are documenting your conversations and that you may have to involve human resources. If your organization uses executive coaches to help employees with developmental issues, hire one to help him stop his behavior. Sit down with the employee who is being victimized and encourage him to stand up for himself. It is also a good idea to meet with both employees at the same time once you've had individual meetings with each person.

If you are less senior: It would be great if you have the confidence to tell this senior person that he is being cruel or unkind, and in theory this is how you should handle the situation. However, this isn't an easy thing to do, so the next best thing to do is to talk to your manager to elicit his help. If your manager is the person who is using humor inappropriately, then talk to human resources. Try very hard not to be intimidated by someone's title or status. There is no excuse for cruelty or ridicule in the workplace.

Someone constantly uses humor to distract others from working.

If you are a peer: If her humor and joking are preventing you from getting your work done, point this out to her. If your coworkers are complaining to you about the jokester's behavior, empathize and encourage them to speak to her directly rather than talking behind her back.

If you are her manager: Gently explain to her that while you enjoy and appreciate her sense of humor, there is a place for joking at work, and a fine line between entertaining coworkers and interfering with their ability to do their jobs.

If you are less senior: Remind her of your business responsibilities and deadlines; behave very businesslike and briskly if necessary; smile politely and turn back to your computer or whatever it is that you are working on. Do this repeatedly, and hopefully she will get the message that she is distracting you. Even if you might slightly offend the person, she can't deny the fact that you are a hard worker.

ASSESS YOUR HUMOR

Just as it is tough for you to deal with a humorless coworker, it's equally difficult for your colleagues to work with you if your sense of humor is lacking or askew. Answer the following questions to assess your ability to use humor effectively. For each statement, respond in the way that best describes you. Work quickly, recording the first response that comes to mind. Use the following scale:

4 = Strongly agree

3 = Agree

2 = Disagree

1 = Strongly disagree

__ 1. I tell jokes and funny stories regularly.

__ 2. I use humor to communicate in many situations.

__ 3. I have a great memory for punch lines.

__ 4. My friends and coworkers would definitely describe me as funny.

__ 5. People usually laugh at my jokes and stories.

__ 6. I am confident about using self-effacing humor.

__ 7. I prefer to be around funny people.

__ 8. I smile and laugh a lot.

__ 9. I believe that humor is important in the workplace.

__ 10. Before I begin a serious conversation, especially at work, I make it a habit to "break the ice" first by joking about something.

__ 11. Even if I don't necessarily understand them, I appreciate all kinds of humor, from juvenile and slapstick to sarcastic and highbrow.

__ 12. I use humor as a coping mechanism for handling tough times and negative situations most of the time.

__ 13. I seek out things that make me laugh, such as renting funny movies, going to the circus, watching sitcoms, and reading jokes.

__ 14. I can remember precisely the last time I laughed so hard I couldn't stand up and tears rolled down my face.

__ 15. When I am involved in a tense or difficult conversation with someone at work, I usually suggest that we try to step back and lighten up.

SCORE KEY

Add up the numbers that you entered for each question. If you scored:

15 to 25—You are a very serious person who finds it difficult to smile, laugh, or take a lighthearted approach to problems and tough situations. Remember that other people find it much easier to communicate with peo-

ple who have a healthy sense of humor. This doesn't mean that you suddenly need to start telling jokes in staff meetings but, instead, that you can really benefit from discovering an appreciation for humor, both your own and other people's.

26 to 37—Somewhere along the line you've lost your ability to laugh, smile, and joke with others. It's time to remember what it feels like to appreciate and express humor again. Using humor can facilitate open communication, build relationships, energize you, improve your attention span, enhance your problem-solving ability, and broaden your perspective.

38 to 48—You have a balanced and appropriate sense of humor. You use humor effectively as a tool for dealing with the unpleasant aspects of life. There are times, though, when you allow stress to overcome you, and you forget to lighten up, taking yourself and others far too seriously. When you catch yourself in this position, take a deep breath and think of a way to interject humor.

49 to 60—You rely on humor to navigate the ups and downs of life. You are widely known as a person with a great sense of humor who likes to laugh and to help others laugh with you. You have a gift, and you enjoy sharing it with others. If your score fell on the high end of this scale, it's possible that you use humor at times when it may not be a suitable way to communicate. Be wary of always hiding behind humor to avoid your fear of being serious when it matters.

If your score fell between 38 and 60 and you feel comfortable with your sense of humor but would still like to learn some tips for interacting with people who take you, and themselves, too seriously and could use a little lightening up, move on to the last section of this chapter (page 158).

If you scored between 15 and 37, or you simply know in your gut that you need to work on your sense of humor and start smiling and laughing more often, read on!

Need to Lighten Up? Complete This Assessment

Before you can work on improving your sense of humor, it would be helpful for you to try to understand what makes you laugh. Ask yourself the following questions and write down your answers:

1. Think of a situation that occurred recently at work or in your personal life that made you laugh and smile both when it happened and afterward. Describe what happened and why it made you laugh.

   _____

   _____

   _____

2. Name the title of your all-time favorite comedy film, and list three reasons why it's your favorite.

   _____

   _____

   _____

3. What is your favorite TV sitcom (past or present)? Why?

   _____

   _____

   _____

4. Who is your favorite comedian? Why?

   _____

   _____

   _____

5. Do you have a favorite newspaper comic strip? If so, what is it and why?

   _____

   _____

   _____

6. Who in your life consistently cheers you up, brings a smile to your face, or makes you chuckle? Why?

   _____

   _____

How easy or difficult was it to answer these questions? Do you see a common theme in your answers? What is it? The most important point of this exercise is for you to be able to identify your personal sources of humor and laughter. If you cannot, is it because you don't expose yourself enough to humor and humorous situations? Are you so entrenched in the serious side of life that you've forgotten how to seek out fun and laughter? If so, not to worry, you may just need a jump start. Maybe you're thinking to yourself, "I can't learn how to be funny. It's just not who I am." Maybe you won't ever be able to tell a joke well, but you can certainly make humor a more significant part of your life. Here are some exercises and suggestions to help you enhance and develop your sense of humor and for working with "humorously challenged" folks.

TIPS AND TECHNIQUES FOR IMPROVING YOUR HUMOR
Develop Your Light Side

Here is a list of actions you can take to generate humor. Check off the ones you're willing to try in the immediate future.

_____ Create a place in your work space that is focused just on humor, such as a bulletin board where you can post cartoons, humorous quotes, jokes, or silly photographs.

_____ Every time you walk past a mirror, smile.

_____ Whenever you see other people, even if they are a strangers, smile at them.

_____ Next time you're stressed out by a tight deadline, a traffic jam, a long line at the bank, or an interminable wait on a customer-service phone hotline, make a silly joke about it to yourself or someone else.

_____ When you make a mistake in front of someone, make a self-effacing joke about it to yourself or someone else.

_____ If you're going through a tough time in your life right now, think about it and write down the humorous aspects of it. If you can't think of anything funny, ask a friend or supportive person to help you look at your situation from a humorous standpoint. (Obviously, if your situation is tragic, this may not be the right time to do this exercise.)

_____ Have a tickling contest with your spouse, significant other, or child. Try to hold out as long as you can.

_____ It's likely that you work with someone who makes other people laugh. Observe that person for two weeks and take notes—literally—on his or her approach to and uses of humor.

While it may seem odd to try to force yourself to be funny or to make other people laugh, sometimes it's a good idea to coax yourself or someone else into a lighter mood. Just as with the other Keys, you may feel that Humor either comes instinctively to you or not. Few people are born possessing all Eleven Keys in perfect amounts. Humor, especially, is one Key that some people seem to come by naturally while others don't. But in reality, this just isn't true. Your openness to enhancing or changing your sense of humor can be a crucial factor in your effectiveness at work. Sometimes, the best kind of humor to use is the kind that pokes fun at yourself.

John, a senior human-resources executive, worked for a Japanese manufacturing company. Not only was he responsible for managing the firm's American employees, he also had to communicate effectively with its Japanese owners.

John tells a story about the time he was presenting a plan for a new performance management and compensation program to a group of Japanese executives. Midway through his presentation, he noticed that there was limited eye contact and lots of fidgeting going on in the audience. He stopped dead and said, "We Americans are like John Wayne, we shoot first and aim later. I ask you for your forgiveness. Obviously, I did not study your culture well enough before I prepared this presentation. Can you help me?"

Everyone in the room laughed uproariously and then gave John their undivided attention. John, a six-foot-five guy with a booming voice, conjured up a visual image of John Wayne that clearly tickled the collective "funny bone" of his Japanese colleagues. He proceeded to finish his presentation, earning immediate approval for the new plan. John explained that while many American businesspeople he knew were afraid to joke with their Japanese counterparts, he constantly used humor as a tool for leveling the playing field. By injecting humor into a potentially disastrous business situation, he took a risk, made himself vulnerable—and human—and was rewarded for his effort.

If you are a habitual jokester or are prone to using humor maliciously or at inappropriate times, then take a few minutes to answer the questions in the following assessment.

Do You Use Humor Inappropriately?

When using humor at work, remember this cardinal rule: Think before you act or open your mouth. Take a moment and think through the potential impact of your joke or comment on the feelings of the other people involved. Use your sense of humor in a positive way, taking care not to direct it at any one individual or group in a derogatory manner. Humorous "clean" jokes, storytelling, "one-liners," anecdotes, and mildly self-deprecating humor are all appropriate types of workplace humor.

It's great to be funny. Who doesn't enjoy the rush that comes with knowing you've made other people laugh? But when we do this to show off or to deflect negative attention from ourselves and onto someone else, we're crossing a dangerous line. Since we're all human and work can be stressful, any of us, at any time, can fall into the habit of making light of certain issues or people without realizing it.

What constitutes inappropriate humor? Jokes that make fun of an individual or group based on their race, ethnicity, religion, age, gender, or sexual preference are always in questionable taste but are a definite no-no in the workplace. Not only is this the case for moral reasons, but there is a danger of lawsuits. Humor that is used at the wrong time, in the wrong situation, or with the wrong individuals present is inappropriate at work ("bathroom" humor, for example). Failing to combine humor with other Keys such as Empathy, Respect, and Optimism can be threatening to people who may not be as confident as you are. Or it can be just plain offensive!

Excessive use of humor is also inappropriate at work. If you are constantly making jokes, your relentless attempts at humor will eventually be viewed by your coworkers as an annoying and tedious play for attention. What you intend to be fun and entertaining may be a time-waster for other people.

On the line below, write down the name of someone you trust who can give you honest feedback about times when you may have inadvertently used humor to overstep the boundaries at work, and offended a coworker.

People who use humor in negative ways are likely to be skilled communicators who misuse their talent. Humorists, like all skilled communicators, are adept at timing. Pacing, pausing, and the strategic use of silence are three components of timing. Think of a recent situation in which you used humor in a way that backfired and which you now regret. Describe the situation, your failed attempt at humor, and the outcome in the space below.

_____

_____

_____

If given a second chance, how could you have turned things around? For example, could you have paused or used silence instead of making flippant quips or using barbs?

_____

_____

_____

Is there someone at work whom you constantly pick on or make the butt of a joke to get other people to laugh? Pretend you are that person. Describe, honestly, how you think your ribbing makes that person feel. If it's easier, just use one-word answers to name the emotions that you imagine the other person experiences (anger, sadness, embarrassment, etc.).

_____

_____

_____

CREATE AN ACTION PLAN

Many people mistakenly assume that humor is a gift that only some people are born with, and that it cannot be learned. Contrary to popular belief, humor is a universal human trait that can be nurtured and cultivated. It is simply more active in some people and dormant in others.

Micki has always been a rather serious person by nature, especially at work. She has been told in performance reviews that she needs to lighten up, but she honestly isn't sure how to do this. When her boss and coworkers joke and laugh in meetings, Micki notices that they usually tend to ignore her because they know from experience that she won't respond. When asked to think about what triggers her sense of humor, she admits that her six-year-old twins are her only real stimulant for laughter. Micki really wants to temper her overly serious demeanor at work, but isn't sure where to start. She needs to write an action plan.

Here is Micki's action plan:

My goal: I am going to smile and laugh more often, respond more frequently to other people's humor, and attempt to use humor myself.

MY SHORT-TERM OBJECTIVES/ACTIVITIES ARE:

1. Smile every time I walk past a mirror or see another person. I've been told I frown a lot, and this is a good start.
2. Rent several movies that represent different styles of comedy and watch them back to back so that I can begin to understand what makes people laugh, and decide what style of humor is funny to me. I will make an effort to be aware of how good I feel when I'm around my children and collapse in gales of laughter.
3. Ask my husband to give me feedback about my sense of humor.

MY MEDIUM-TERM OBJECTIVES/ACTIVITIES ARE:

1. Learn two jokes and tell them at the next staff meeting. I don't expect to become a skilled joke teller, but I think it will help me to appreciate other people when they tell jokes.
2. Write down three recent examples of how funny my kids are, and share anecdotes with one or two people at work with whom I feel comfortable.

MY LONG-TERM OBJECTIVE/ACTIVITY IS:

1. Take a comedy class. This scares me to death, but I think it will do wonders for my self-confidence and enable me to have fun exploring and developing my sense of humor.

Now, fill out your own action plan. Keep it simple, just like Micki did.

My goal:
_____
_____

My short-term objectives/activities are:
_____
_____
By when: _____

My medium-term objectives/activities are:
_____
_____
By when: _____

My long-term objectives/activities are:
_____
_____
By when: _____

Want to get more satisfaction from work, improve your job performance, and get along with your colleagues? Then lighten up, smile, joke, and laugh as often as possible. And by all means, share your sense of humor with others. But heed these words of caution: Never use humor as a weapon, especially in the workplace. Employ your sense of humor as the valuable communication tool that it can and *should* be. The benefits you reap will give you something to smile about. Using Humor effectively is instrumental in building relationships with people you work with, networking with people outside your company, generating sales, and nurturing clients.

Key #7:
Intelligence

It is unwise to be too sure of one's own wisdom.
It is healthy to be reminded that the strongest
might weaken and the wisest might err.

—MOHANDAS K. GANDHI

The Intelligence Key is not the same as the intelligence that is measured by an IQ test. "Intelligence" is defined in *The American Heritage Dictionary* as "the capacity to acquire and apply knowledge" and "the ability to think and reason." While a person's ability to do these things is certainly important on the job, what's even more significant is his or her possession of creativity, wisdom, common sense, and social sensitivity. When a colleague is missing one or several of these elements of Intelligence, the frustration it can cause for you is monumental. If we were to break these categories down further to practical competencies and qualities, a person who possesses all the elements of the Intelligence Key has the ability to:

- **Solve problems**—Identifying effective solutions for difficult problems; seeing underlying or hidden patterns; being good at analysis and looking beyond the obvious. Most people are presented with problems at work on a regular basis. If it's a problem that occurs repeatedly, it becomes a habit to solve it. If, however, it's a new type of problem, the need to use a problem-solving model becomes necessary. Regardless of what your job is, you are expected to solve problems, in many cases, with limited input from your boss or colleagues. And, of course, clients depend on you to solve their problems efficiently and effectively as this is what they are paying you to do. When someone isn't a skilled problem solver, this impacts everyone on the team who is relying on him.

- **Be creative**—Taking original, imaginative, even innovative approaches to processes, projects, concepts, and problems at work; being able to connect unrelated ideas or concepts. The complexity of the workplace causes problems to be solved, challenges to be overcome, and opportunities to be leveraged. While some people seem to naturally be creative, creativity, like all the elements of the Intelligence Key, can be learned. In *Breakthrough Thinking,* authors Gerald Nadler and Shozo Hibino state, "Simply copying someone else's methods guarantees we will remain behind. For even as we rush to adapt, our competitors are themselves making changes and improvements in their methods, changes certain to put them in front again, just when we assume we have at last become competitive by our rapid implementation of their now outmoded methods." It's not difficult to understand how creativity applies to business, or how uninspiring it is to work with someone who isn't creative. Not only is it dull and tedious to work with a noncreative person, it becomes frustrating when a new solution or approach is a necessity for achieving business results.

- **Possess a larger perspective**—Seeing the broadest possible view of an issue or problem; being able to look into the future while not losing sight of the present or past. The more senior you are, the greater the expectation is that you make decisions and take action strategically and with vision. This means balancing context, experience, and information. When you first become a manager, it is easiest to rely on your technical knowledge and abilities to get things done. When your responsibilities become more expansive, this approach is dangerously shortsighted. If you're a receptionist, your job is structured and can be managed tactically. If, however, you are managing a department, the need to gain a greater perspective becomes even more necessary because of the many people, projects, and priorities you face every day. A colleague who insists on staying mired in the day-to-day details of something, instead of seeing the greater view, can strongly inhibit your ability to implement.

- **Communicate effectively**—Passing information from one person to another through speaking, writing, listening, and running meetings with the intention of achieving a specific result. Communication skills are important in any situation where people interact. Work is no exception. If someone is unable to listen well, articulate a focused message, and give and accept feedback, you will surely experience confusion and conflict with your colleagues and clients. Working with a poor communicator is irksome and counterproductive.

- **Execute**—Carrying out strategy, plans, and goals and performing well while doing so. It's great to possess a big-picture perspective and to put a plan with corresponding goals in place—but if you don't make it all happen, these elements won't matter. Scores of factors can interfere with execution: Having the "wrong" people on your team, not putting a solid strategy or approach in place, failing to get support from "stakeholders," neglecting to create an action plan with specific goals, failing to follow up consistently, and avoiding dealing with problems immediately as they arise. If a colleague isn't able to implement and fulfill a plan of action, his coworkers will have to compensate for this lack of Intelligence by taking on more than their share of the load.

POINTERS FOR WORKING WITH PEOPLE WHO LACK (ONE OR MORE ASPECTS OF) INTELLIGENCE

Just as it's rare for you to possess just the right amount of each of the elements of Intelligence, it's likely that you work with people who lack specific aspects, which can be infuriating at times. Here are some ideas for learning how to deal more effectively with them regardless of what your relationship is.

Someone panics when she confronts a problem at work and, instead of handling it, relies on you or your colleagues to solve it.

If you are a peer: The next time she has a panic attack about a problem, sit down with her and try to help her get to the root of her emotional reaction. Is her confidence shaky or is she unsure how to handle a problem? Maybe she's afraid to make a decision for fear that it will be the wrong one. Whatever her feelings are, it's necessary to understand

---

RELATED KEYS 🔑━━

KEY #7: INTELLIGENCE

🔑━ **Curiosity** about yourself, your job, your organization, and your industry helps you to gain information and knowledge so that you can solve problems, delegate well, possess a greater perspective, and execute—some of the crucial elements of the Intelligence Key.

🔑━ **Confidence and Intelligence** are closely related for the simple reason that Intelligence requires learning, understanding, growing, change, and achievement, all which are difficult to achieve without a healthy and realistic outlook.

🔑━ **Decisiveness** is the backbone for time management, organization, and plan execution. Many aspects of Intelligence involve taking different approaches and taking risks. Without the ability to make decisions constantly, you will be unable to take the most intelligent approaches in your work.

🔑━ **Flexibility** is an ingredient necessary to communicate well and certainly to taking creative approaches to problems, processes, and concepts.

🔑━ **Self-awareness** is needed to understand your own strengths, weaknesses, and abilities so that you can demonstrate the many elements of Intelligence at work.

---

them before being able to help her. Be reassuring and offer to role-play with her the actions she can take. Obviously, one of your motives for helping her learn to solve problems with composure is to curb her dependence on you. If you've done this several times and she continues to freak out over problems, slowly begin to be less available to help her. Assure her that you have complete confidence in her ability to problem-solve.

If you are her manager: It's especially helpful to understand what's at the root of her problem-solving panic if she reports to you. Once you realize what's causing her paralysis or uncertainty, you can focus your encouragement on helping her overcome whatever it is. Recommend a problem-solving model and ask her to use it next time while communicating her progress to you along the way.

If you are less senior: It's really frustrating to have to rely on a senior manager who doesn't solve problems smoothly. While you'll need to be careful not to show your frustration, when you see that she is struggling with a problem, offer to help by suggesting specific things you can do. It's tough to coach a senior person, but if you put yourself in the position of helping her to alleviate her problem-solving stress, perhaps she'll grow more confident.

Someone just doesn't ever look at her work through a different lens. Instead, she takes the least original, least imaginative approach to projects, problems, and processes.

If you are a peer: When you are working on a project or task together, ask her if she would mind brainstorming ways that you could handle the situation differently. If she protests, ask her to humor you and spend some time brainstorming anyway. If she pushes back, delicately give her feedback that her lack of creativity inhibits change and getting things done productively.

If you are her manager: Tell her that you've identified a specific responsibility or project and that you'd like to ask her to approach it differently than she has in the past. Explain that you are very interested in achieving business results with minimal risk; however, you are sure that there could be a more creative way to do so. Encourage her to attend a creativity seminar or conference (such as one offered by Creative Education Foundation—cef-cpsi.org) or buy books on how to become creative at work. Maybe you could even bring an outside trainer in to teach a creativity class.

If you are less senior: Think of a process or project that has always been handled the same way, and do your homework about how it could be handled more creatively. Set up a meeting with your higher-up and explain why you believe your approach is more innovative yet would produce better results. She may resist. If she does, don't give up. Keep thinking of different approaches and keep showing her what they are. Perhaps she will come around and begin to approach her job more creatively or at least allow you to.

Someone stays focused on the details of a situation instead of looking broadly at future implications and identifying a more strategic, less tactical view.

If you are a peer: Being a real visionary is one of the toughest competencies to learn. If you believe that this is one of your strengths, you'd be doing your colleague a big favor by working alongside him to show him how he can learn to gain a larger perspective. Naturally, if your shortsighted coworker isn't open to or interested in learning this particular element of Intelligence, you can't force him.

If you are his manager: If you sit down with your employee and tell him that you'd like him to become more strategic, it's likely that he'll nod at you, leave your office, and approach his job the same as ever. Instead, outline the benefits of having a broader perspective, such as the ability to see ahead clearly; accurately anticipate future consequences and trends; visualize and articulate a credible picture of possibilities and likelihoods; and create competitive strategies and plans. Give him an example of a work situation you've been involved in where your approach was strategic, and explain how you handled it. Encourage him to view his job similarly, and coach him over time.

If you are less senior: Most employees expect the leadership of their company to be strategic, and it's disappointing when it isn't. If your manager takes a tactical and micro approach to something, ask him a series of questions about his vision, the future implications of his decisions, and why he expects his strategy to work. Obviously, you'll have to word your questions very diplomatically so that he doesn't feel that you are challenging his authority. If you have ideas for taking a strategic approach about a project you're involved with, by all means share them with him.

Someone doesn't prioritize well, value his own time or anyone else's, or use systems and technology efficiently.

If you are a peer: Everyone struggles with time management at work, including you. It's likely that your coworker demonstrates a pattern of behavior such as always being late in providing information to you or being late to meetings you run. Sit him down and tell him how overwhelmed you are at times, and ask him if he feels the same way. If he agrees, ask him if there is something he can do to be more considerate of your time, using a specific situation as feedback. Be sure to offer your support and assistance. Offer suggestions for how he can change, or mention that you've read a few good books on how to manage time.

If you are his manager: If you've gotten actual complaints from your employee's coworkers about his poor time-management skills, you can sit down and ask him about the substance and context. Let him explain his perspective of his time management. If he admits that he mismanages his or his colleague's time, make some suggestions about how he can handle his time more effectively. Encourage him to buy a book or take a class on time management. Ask him to share the ways he's going to behave differently with the coworker whose time he is misusing. Be sure he is aware that his lack of skills is affecting his colleagues and building resentment.

If you are less senior: Sometimes a senior manager forgets about all the people who depend on him to make decisions and provide information in a timely way so that they can get their work done. If a senior person at your company is constantly abusing your time, hard as it is to do, you must say something to him. The easiest approach is for you to tell him that you are missing your deadlines (or whatever else affects your work) and you'd like to know how you can help him so that this will not continue to happen. You're probably not going to be able to give him time-management tips unless he is open to hearing them.

Someone is a very unfocused and confusing communicator in meetings, e-mail, and memos.

If you are a peer: Most people become accustomed to communicating in a certain way and may not realize that they can change or improve the way they relay information. If your colleague is unclear, ask him questions to help clarify and to explain what he's saying in a different way by using other words, phrases, examples, or visual descriptions.

If you are his manager: Your direct report may not even be aware that he is not communicating well. If this is so, your first step is to give him some very specific examples of ways in which you are confused by the way he conveys or presents information. Instead of telling him how to communicate better, ask him to give you ways that he thinks he can improve the way he communicates. Ask him to create a development plan with goals and ways to learn, and share it with you. Give him regular feedback about his communication in e-mail, meetings, and memos.

If you are less senior: You can certainly ask him for clarification about what he's said or written so that you can understand it. However, this won't help your situation long-term because he may not know how confusing he can be and will likely continue to communicate the same way. So, you may want to take a deep breath, sit down with him, and tell him that you're often left confused about what he says. If you don't have the courage to do this, then remember that misunderstandings due to poor communication can lead to even bigger problems.

Someone never seems to bring a project to fruition, meet deadlines, or reach the desired business outcome that was originally outlined. In other words, she doesn't make things happen.

If you are a peer: No doubt, if you are concerned about your coworker's inability to execute, it must be affecting you in some way. Ask her if you can meet to discuss your interdependence and the ways that you can improve the results together. If she gets defensive, explain that you are missing your deadline (or whatever the issue is) and you really want to prevent this from happening again. Ask her if she can walk you through her process for getting results so you might make suggestions for improvement. If she remains resistant to your help, it's time to get your manager involved.

If you are her manager: Ask your direct report if she is satisfied with the results she's getting. Whether or not she is, tell her that you're disappointed in her inability to execute. Create a development plan with checkpoints when she'll have to share her progress with you. Time management, a lack of clarity about the expected outcome, indecisiveness, low confidence, and poor communication skills are all possible reasons for your employee's inability to execute. She needs to understand that everyone is expected to achieve business results, and she's no exception.

If you are less senior: A leader who doesn't execute is a lame duck. Eventually, most managers and executives will derail if they don't set the wheels of motion forward and get expected results. Be impeccable at documenting your goals, actions, and overall contribution to getting business results in the event that you become part of the scrutiny. This is all information you'll need for your résumé as well, so it's a good exercise (you should always have an updated résumé so you don't have to scramble when you really need one).

The more aware you are of how balanced your own Intelligence Key is, the better able you will be to work with others who lack one or more of the five elements of the Key.

ASSESS YOUR INTELLIGENCE

Answer the following questions to help you assess whether or not you display the elements of Intelligence. Circle the letter that best describes how you typically react or behave in the situation. Record your immediate impression.

1. When you are faced with a problem at work that you've never encountered before, you:
   a. Feel anxious and delay trying to come up with a solution.
   b. Request an urgent meeting with your boss to discuss it.
   c. Identify some possible solutions and then run them by someone whom you trust at work who's dealt with the same problem before.
   d. Approach the problem using *c,* and then plug all the information into a problem-solving model.

2. Creativity at work to you means:
   a. Thinking about how to solve a problem in a different way but usually in your spare time.
   b. Generating lots of ideas before you solve a problem.
   c. Scheduling "creative time" on your calendar.
   d. Restructuring your time so that you spend more time on innovation, seeking new approaches and making ongoing improvements in things.

3. Possessing a broad and visionary perspective:
   a. Is something that should be left to the CEO or president of your organization.
   b. Seems important but you just don't have the time because of all the fires you have to put out every day.
   c. Is something you have experienced at times and would really like to work on developing into a stronger ability.
   d. Is a trait you are proud to possess even during the most stressful situations and times.

4. Whether you are reading an e-mail, participating in a meeting, or talking to someone in the hallway, you:

a. Can't help daydreaming and thinking about all the work you have to do, instead of focusing 100 percent on the person talking or writing.

b. Try hard to listen and pay attention to the message the other person is conveying.

c. Keep working at improving your ability to communicate effectively.

d. Pride yourself on listening actively, sending simple and clear e-mails and not wasting anyone's time regardless of the method you are using to communicate.

5. When it comes to completing projects and implementing plans:

a. You rely on your coworkers for this because your real strength is analysis and strategy.

b. You get started but sometimes lose steam and don't finish by the deadline or fail to achieve the best results.

c. When you're interested in something, you make it happen and achieve good results (this is most of the time), but occasionally you stop short of finishing something.

d. Your reputation is unparalleled for getting things done regardless of the obstacles along the way *and* doing a stellar job.

SCORE KEY

Each of the questions you answered represents one of the five elements of the Intelligence Key.

Check the answer that was your response.

Question 1—Solving problems   a __ b __ c __ d __

If you selected *a* or *b*, you could benefit from learning a simple problem-solving model to use the next time you're faced with an unfamiliar or perplexing issue. Choosing *c* or *d* means that you're comfortable with your ability to solve problems.

Question 2—Being creative   a __ b __ c __ d __

Answering *a* or *b* indicates that you may spend more of your time "putting out fires" than thinking of new and innovative approaches to situations and problems at work. If your response was *c* or *d*, you have figured out how important it is to infuse your work with creativity.

Question 3—Possessing a larger perspective   a __ b __ c __ d __

Perspective is a mix of vision, strategy, and common sense. This is one of the more complicated elements of Intelligence, and if you selected *a* or *b*, you haven't yet recognized the tremendous value that a broad perspective can give you. Choosing *c* or *d* doesn't necessarily mean that you possess a greater perspective, but it does mean that you appreciate the benefit perspective can bring to your decision-making.

Question 4—Communicating effectively   a __ b __ c __ d __

The most significant cause of productivity and relationship breakdowns at work is poor communication. You spend so much time communicating that it's imperative that you continually sharpen your speaking and writing skills. If you answered *a* or *b* for this question, this is probably a real developmental need for you. Choosing *c* or *d* is a good sign that you consider communication skills to be important.

Question 5—Executing   a __ b __ c __ d __

If you are analytical and thoughtful in your approach at work, you may not be as action oriented, and vice versa. But executing isn't just about reaching a result; it is also about performing well during the process and getting the *best* results. Answering *a* or *b* indicates a need to work on executing. Chose *c* or *d*? Good for you!

If you chose *a* or *b* answers for three or more of the five questions, you have some significant work to do to improve your Intelligence overall.

TIPS AND TECHNIQUES FOR IMPROVING YOUR INTELLIGENCE
Which Aspects of Intelligence Would You Like to Develop?

Based upon your answers to the questions above, choose the aspects of Intelligence that are developmental needs for you. Read below what you can do to improve these.

Solving Problems

Problems tend to involve patterns that are a composite of similar traits or characteristics. For example: Ed is a municipal traffic engineer and has been called in to observe traffic patterns (no pun intended!) at an intersection in town. He sees that the intersection gets clogged every day at 8 a.m. and 3 p.m. After scouting the surrounding area, he notices a middle school nearby with a small parking lot. Because of the limited parking space, parents drop their kids off and pick them up at the busy intersection, where they walk to and from the school. This holds up the regular traffic flow in the intersection. While Ed was able to quickly diagnose the problem by observing the situation, he still needed to come up with a solution. He decided to use a five-step problem-solving model using questions. Here it is:

What is the problem? Describe it as completely as possible.
There is too much traffic in the intersection at two specific times of the day.

What is the scale or severity of the problem?
This creates a bottleneck and forces drivers to sit through two or three light changes before moving through the intersection. As a result, accidents and incidents of "road rage" have been higher than normal.

What is the current situation?
Drivers are managing the problem themselves by speeding and driving recklessly. There's simply too much traffic in the intersection during peak times. The mayor and the town residents are growing concerned.

What is the ideal situation?
Parents need a different place to drop off and pick up their kids. The timing of the lights should be adjusted so that traffic flow will move more rapidly through the intersection.

What actions need to be taken?
Get approval for the construction of a circular drive in front of the school so that parents can discharge their kids there instead of in the intersection.
Analyze the timing of the light changes and recommend that the timing be adjusted to handle the traffic surges.
Now, *you* try it with a problem you're facing at work.

What is the problem? Describe it as completely as possible.

_____
_____
_____

What is the scale or severity of the problem?

_____
_____
_____

What is the current situation?

_____
_____
_____

What is the ideal situation?

_____
_____
_____

What actions need to be taken?

_____
_____
_____

Several things to remember about solving problems:

- Stay open-minded.
- Be sure that you have correct and sufficient data about the situation, but don't overanalyze it either.
- Always gain commitment from everyone involved in the situation.

The more often you tackle a problem logically and systematically, the more comfortable you will feel solving problems, and the results you achieve will be the best possible.

BEING CREATIVE

People who take creative approaches share many of the same qualities. They *believe* that they are creative; they are confident (see Key #1: Confidence), curious (see Key #2: Curiosity), flexible (see Key #5: Flexibility), and perseverant (see Key #9: Perseverance). Unfortunately, the typical workplace, with its sterility and structure, does little to nurture creativity. This means that you must continually motivate yourself to be creative so that it becomes more natural. Here are some suggestions for doing so:

- Explore nature—Go on a hike, climb a mountain, walk at the beach, or explore a forest. Doing so will awaken all your senses, restore your vitality, and stimulate your imagination.
- Exercise regularly—Working out physically eases stress, raises your stamina, and increases your energy level—not to mention improving the oxygen flow to your brain!
- Enjoy different experiences—Take a hot-air balloon ride, go scuba diving, sit under a bridge and listen to the cars, go to the circus, or visit a zoo. Doing these things will pull you out of your everyday world and remind you of the extraordinary parts of the world that you might have forgotten.
- Brainstorm with others—Schedule time with your friends and family to generate creative ideas for a problem you're having, a new business you'd like to start, or anything else that is stumping you. True brainstorming isn't structured; everyone throws out as many ideas as they can without judgment from the other group members.
- Go somewhere and be quiet—in *Thinkertoys: A Handbook of Business Creativity for the '90s,* Michael Michalko suggests "quieting your mind so that you can see the solutions that are already there." He suggests meditating, emptying your mind of all thoughts, or sitting in a comfortable, peaceful place for fifteen minutes without falling asleep.

Creativity is not just restricted to artists and musicians. Creativity can and *should* be used in every aspect of business. Try a few of these suggestions and you'll be pleasantly surprised at how well your creative juices will flow.

POSSESSING A LARGER PERSPECTIVE

Someone who can "see the big picture" is able to understand the details of the situation, remember the past, *and* look into the future. Having a larger perspective is a wonderful tool for anticipating and solving problems, creating new products and services, and planning and setting goals. Take the example of Roxanne. As the new practice manager in a veterinary hospital, she has been hired to turn the hospital around. Revenues are down, seven doctors have quit, and theft is high—the problems are endless. The first thing Roxanne did was identify the fundamental areas in the hospital, such as client service, the practice of medicine, facility management, etc. She then created a chart describing the characteristics that would exist if everything was perfect. Next, she interviewed everyone in the hospital to identify their skills, experiences, responsibilities, and attitudes and to get feedback about what was happening. She then did a gap analysis between the ideal state and what was really going on. Unfortunately, she had to fire some people because of their poor attitudes or resistance to change. In an off-site meeting with key employees, everyone created a mission and vision of the ideal state of the hospital six months ahead.

Roxanne assigned a "champion" to take charge of each area of the hospital from animal boarding to laundry to the reception area to ultrasounds. She set goals and expectations with each person and, based upon his or her input, started making decisions about changing things and spending money. Now you try it. What significant problem or issue are you facing in your job right now? Write down the answers to each question:

What is the actual problem or situation? Be specific and descriptive.

_____

_____

_____

How can you break the problem or situation down into subcategories? What are they?

_____

_____

_____

What is the history of the situation (going back two to five years)?

_____

_____

_____

If the problem was resolved or the situation improved, what would this look like? (What is the ideal state?) Describe it.

_____

_____

_____

Who are all the people involved right now? These are "stakeholders"—anyone who has any kind of impact on the situation, even if it's minimal. What exactly is their involvement or connection with the situation?

_____

_____

_____

Do you know what each person's skills, experience, attitude, and insight are in the situation? Write each person's name down and list these things.

_____

_____

_____

Conduct a gap analysis. In the example above, Roxanne learned that laundry piled up, sometimes for two weeks. This resulted in rats nesting in the laundry room and the animals not having clean blankets. The gap is that there needed to be enough clean blankets every day and no one person had been accountable just for doing laundry. Write your gap analysis.

_____

_____

_____

Who can you identify to help or coach you to achieve the ideal state?

_____

_____

_____

What can you do to prevent this problem from happening in the future?

_____

_____

_____

Not only is this a formula for gaining a bigger perspective, it is also a great problem-solving model. Gaining a larger perspective requires the right amount of fact-finding and analysis combined with intuition and understanding history and future implications.

COMMUNICATE EFFECTIVELY

We underestimate the amount of time wasted on poor communication. The best communicators are articulate and take the time to learn what is important to the other person *and* communicate using the most effective method, whether it's e-mail, the phone, or a meeting.

Publishing coach Lucy Hedrick is the author of *Get Organized in the Digital Age*. She has a few observations about the telephone and meetings: "A frequent complaint people make is about callers who perpetuate 'telephone tag,' or the lengthy cycle of voice mails that accomplish nothing. Telephone productivity is increased when callers actually imagine that they will never talk live. In other words, pretend you're only going to communicate by voice mail, but you have to move your agenda forward. It's amazing how detailed and specific your voice mails become!"

As for meetings (one of the most abused business rituals in corporate America), Hedrick says, "If you struggle to start your meetings on time and your participants routinely straggle in, put a period of time for schmoozing at the top of the agenda. This lets people see that 8:45 to 9:00 a.m., for example, they can come in, take their coats off, grab a cup of coffee, ask about someone's weekend, and so on. But at 9:00 a.m., the gavel comes down!" Hedrick advises, "Don't call a meeting just to pass along information—you can do that electronically or one-on-one."

Truly effective communicators possess three traits:

1. They possess empathy. Read about Key #4: Empathy to learn how to develop Empathy to improve your relationships with people at work.

2. They create trust. Trust means that you are reliable and that you possess integrity. It means that you have expertise. Your expertise can be your knowledge, your credentials, or your experience. This gives you credibility, which makes you believable. Being believable means that what you say or write is accepted as the truth and that you come across as sincere and genuine. In other words, it means that whoever you are communicating with has the confidence that your message has veracity.

   Credibility also has to do with automatic authority. Authority can be organizational—your title and position may give you power—or it can be legal, it can be related to associations you have with people who are credible, it can be related to status, or you can be an elected official. These kinds of authority may give you credibility initially, but they are not enough to persuade people long-term if integrity and trustworthiness are absent.

3. They are strong listeners. Research conducted by Lominger Inc., a leadership-development consulting firm based in Minneapolis, identified listening as the strongest "compensator skill" that can be used (a skill or characteristic that can balance or compensate for overused strengths) and also as a "saving-grace skill" (like humor, integrity, trust, interpersonal savvy, compassion, approachability, and relationships with your managers).

Tips for being a better listener:

- Be present! Daydreaming is the single greatest barrier to active listening.
- Build rapport by mirroring and pacing the person speaking.
- Control your emotions and don't let someone push your hot buttons.
- Control distractions (e-mail!).
- Attend to the feelings of the person who's talking, not just to the content of what he or she is saying.
- When disagreeing, summarize what you have heard before responding with your point of view.
- Avoid interrupting people; wait until they have finished making their points.
- Keep an open mind. We all say that we have an open mind, but the truth can be different.
- Check whether you have understood the speaker by paraphrasing or asking questions.
- Encourage the other person by nodding and using neutral words and phrases like "Really?" "Oh," "Yes," "Tell me more," or "Go ahead."

Remember that the person who listens is the person who is in better control of the situation, not the speaker. The average person can listen to approximately 500 words per minute, but only speak about 125 words per minute.

Executing

There are three phases to executing:

- **Understanding the project or assignment**—Its goal, background, the people and resources you'll have, the timeline, and the reward or punishment involved if it's successful or not.
- **Creating a strategy**—Consider the people involved, the paths you'll take to make things happen, risk assessment (what could go wrong?), and an outline of how the project will unwind.
- **Implementing**—Keep yourself and your colleagues motivated, handle problems as they occur, and keep stakeholders in the loop about what's happening.

Bruce's boss, Lee, has requested that he create a leadership institute for high-potential employees at their organization. Bruce has never tackled something of this magnitude, so he plans on using the steps outlined above. After sitting down with Lee and interviewing him to learn why he wants a leadership institute and the specifics about timeline, expectations, money, and people, Bruce learned that Lee's boss, the company president, is championing this idea. Bruce organized three strategy meetings with his team and identified the most logical approach, along with each staff member's accountability. During the year it took to design the institute and make it operational, Bruce played the roles of cheerleader, coach, ditch digger, engineer, town crier, and disciplinarian. At his company's annual meeting, Bruce received an excellence award for outstanding accomplishment of the year.

How about *you*? Is there a project or assignment that you must execute? Write it down and start gathering information and preparing to follow the steps of execution outlined above.

Understanding the project or assignment

_____

_____

_____

Creating a strategy

_____

_____

_____

Implementing

_____

_____

_____

DO YOU OVERUSE INTELLIGENCE?

While it's quite unlikely that you possess perfect amounts of all five elements of the Intelligence Key, it's even more unusual to possess too much of each one. You may well overuse problem solving or creativity. If so, step back and ask people close to you how this affects them and their work.

CREATE AN ACTION PLAN

Enrique knows that he panics when any kind of problem pops up at work. Unfortunately, he's the manager of his department and he's well aware that his employees feel as if they can't count on him when the going gets rough. This makes him feel bad, and his manager is starting to wonder if Enrique is in over his head in his job. Enrique wants to develop an action plan for handling problems more smoothly. Here is his action plan:

My goal: I am going to come up with a process for solving problems smoothly.

MY SHORT-TERM OBJECTIVE/ACTIVITY:
1. I am going to interview Joel and Rob in logistics about how they solve problems because they seem so skilled at doing so.

MY MEDIUM-TERM OBJECTIVES/ACTIVITIES:
1. My manager, Skip, used to work in my job before he was promoted. I'm going to ask him for some suggestions about solving the typical problems that occur in my job.
2. I will also ask him to give me feedback about how I am doing.

MY LONG-TERM OBJECTIVES/ACTIVITIES:
1. I will put together a thorough plan and show it to Skip for approval.
2. I will ask my direct reports how they think I am doing.

Now, fill out your own action plan, keeping it simple, just like Enrique did.

My goal:

_____

_____

My short-term objectives/activities:

_____

_____

_____

By when: _____

My medium-term objectives/activities:

_____

_____

_____

By when: _____

My long-term objectives/activities:

_____

_____

_____

By when: _____

Success at work and with other people is not about how hard you work but about how "smart" you work. This means being efficient and effective in your job. Commonly, people who possess the Intelligence Key believe they work for themselves, even if someone is paying their salary. It's easy to hand over psychological control of your goals and actions to those who employ you. Believing that you work for yourself and are accountable for your own results is a significant quality that intelligent people possess.

The Intelligence Key is complex yet easy to understand and learn. As Sophocles said, "Wisdom is the supreme part of happiness."

Key #8:
Optimism

Optimism is the essential quality for doing anything that's hard . . .
that doesn't mean that you're blind or unrealistic, it means you
keep focused on eliminating your risks, modifying your strategy,
until it is a strategy that you can be genuinely optimistic about.

—JEFF BEZOS,
FOUNDER OF AMAZON.COM

Optimists view the world through a lens of possibility. However, true optimism goes deeper than just looking at everything in a positive light—it affects how we think of the *causes* of both the good and bad things that happen to us. The findings are clear: Optimists tend to be healthier, happier, and more successful than other people, and they live longer. Pessimists, on the other hand, are more likely to be prone to stress, excessive worry, inactivity, and poor health.

Psychologist Martin Seligman, considered to be the leading expert on optimism, believes that optimists and pessimists differ in the way that they explain life's events. An optimist explains the cause of "good life events" as being stable, global, and internal (e.g., "I succeeded because I worked hard at it"), and the cause of "bad life events" as being unstable, local, and external (e.g., "I didn't come in first place in the contest because the judges only assessed some of my abilities, not all of them"). A pessimist's reactions are exactly opposite, and the pessimistic person will tend to experience setbacks and suffer longer when bad things happen.

An age-old debate: Are optimists born or made? A pessimist will argue that optimists are born, while an optimist will claim they are made. What's *your* opinion?

RELATED KEYS 🔑——

Key #8: Optimism

🔑 **Confidence** requires courage, clarity, and focus, and enables you to deal with whatever situations life throws your way, including the curveballs.

🔑 **Curiosity** arms you with information, ideas, and new perspectives that will make you more likely to dwell on the most positive and hopeful aspects of any situation.

🔑 **Flexibility** gives you the ability to adapt and respond to change and keep your positive outlook from becoming negative.

🔑 **Humor** is a magic potion for dispelling dark thoughts and restoring a more positive perspective.

🔑 **Perseverance** is the Key that makes things happen. Without this proactive force to help make it reality, positive thinking may stay stuck in the thought stage.

Arlette grew up on a farm in Iowa. She describes the life of a farmer as one of an eternal optimist. Her father and brother have lost entire crops because of weather, insects, and economic recessions. Nevertheless, Arlette has never heard a pessimistic word from either of them. They always believe that despite anything bad that happens to destroy their livelihood, there will always be another season of crops.

When you're optimistic, you'll be more motivated, productive, and energetic. Other people will respond favorably to your enthusiasm by wanting to work with you. Your positive attitude is likely to be infectious and may help your team to perform at higher levels, increasing your organization's overall productivity. If, on the other hand, you meet someone for the first time at work and fail to project a positive attitude, you risk the possibility of that person forming a negative first impression of you—an impression that may be lasting, unless you're lucky enough to get a "second chance" and an opportunity to undo it.

If you're chronically negative in your dealings with colleagues or clients, management will eventually pick up on your attitude. Needless to say, such an attitude won't do much for your future growth with the company. Just as your coworkers are interested in working with someone who is optimistic, when you are stuck having to work with a sourpuss colleague, it makes dealing with her very tedious.

If you're generally a positive thinker, it's tough to deal with individuals who don't share your optimistic outlook. It can be especially frustrating to work with a chronically negative person on a project or toward a common goal. Negative thinking is the bane of creativity. When a new idea or suggestion is presented for consideration, the pessimist will say "But . . ." while the optimist says "And . . ."

Strong relationships are the key to success in business, and negative people tend to have trouble building healthy relationships. Optimism in business fosters collaboration, creativity, and a more open and trusting workplace. Pessimism in business can be powerful, too, but in the opposite way! Unhappy employees make for unhappy customers. Even the most stalwart optimist may be temporarily beaten down in a work environment that breeds negativity. In his book *The Power of Positive Thinking in Business,* Scott Ventrella lists thirty-five work situations that can trigger negative thoughts and attitudes in otherwise optimistic people. Here are some examples he cites: being left out of decisions or plans, company politics, insufficient communication, differences in personal/managerial styles, and receiving performance reviews or feedback. Ventrella recommends pinpointing the events that tend to turn you from an optimist to a pessimist, and reorienting your thoughts when you find that one of your "hot buttons" is being pushed.

Some pessimists proudly claim that they are simply "realists" who view life as it really is. They believe that true optimists are in denial about reality. According to Dr. Martin Seligman, there are appropriate times to use Optimism and situations when it doesn't apply. Optimism is helpful in situations where you need to achieve a goal, or when you are concerned that your negative feelings will steer you off course. If you want to inspire others or lead other people, or if your physical health is threatened, Optimism can be a powerful tool. On the other hand, when planning something risky or very uncertain, it's important to have a solid strategy in place first, *then* become optimistic about it. When you're coaching or counseling someone whose future is dim, being unduly optimistic isn't a good idea either.

Here's the rule of thumb for using the Optimism Key: If the likelihood of failure is high, then Optimism is unrealistic. If the likelihood of failure is low to medium, Optimism may help to turn things around and ensure a positive outcome.

POINTERS FOR WORKING WITH PEOPLE WHO LACK OPTIMISM

Someone frequently makes negative comments about everyone and everything around him.

If you are a peer: Ask him to lunch and tell him there's something important you need to talk with him about, privately and confidentially. When the moment is right, ask him politely to listen to you without responding. Then explain that you find it difficult to work with him because of his negative attitude, and that while you wouldn't want to speak for your coworkers, his nonstop negative comments really dampen morale. If he reacts defensively or makes a negative comment, point out to him that this is exactly what you're talking about. Your suggestions will vary depending upon how seriously he takes your feedback. If he appears to be interested in what you have to say, ask him if he'd find it helpful for you to point out to him (privately) any negative comments you hear him make in the future. If he resists, drop the idea.

If you are his manager: Explain to him that you have expectations about what your employee's attitudes should be and that he is not meeting these. Elaborate by telling him that you understand that everyone has an off day and that the challenges of work can be difficult at times, however, you expect your staff to put a positive spin on as much as they can. Tell him that people generally don't want to be with someone who is negative because it's an energy drainer. Ask him what is causing him to make negative comments.

If you are less senior: Each time this higher-up makes a negative comment, counter with something positive without sounding argumentative. Repeat this behavior so that he realizes that you refuse to let his negativism affect you.

Someone constantly whines and complains.
If you are a peer:
- Joke with her and ask her to say something positive every time she complains.
- Pull her aside and tell her that there is someone with whom you work closely who complains all the time and you'd like her advice about how to deal with this person.
- Avoid complaining or whining back. This kind of communication is sneakily contagious.
- Counter her negative comments with positive ones.
- Acknowledge her complaint and point out one positive thing. Ted and Miranda are cube mates, and practically everything out of Miranda's mouth is a complaint. Recently, Ted decided to try this technique. Here's how the conversation went:
    Miranda: "I am so tired of writing these stupid reports."
    Ted: "I can understand why you feel like this, but you sure are good at writing them. In fact, I'd appreciate it if you could show me a few shortcuts."
    Miranda: "Really? Well, sure, what would you like me to help you with? But I can't do it now because, as usual, I'm totally overworked."

Ted: "I'm so glad you'll help me. You know the reason you feel overworked is because Joe (their boss) trusts you the most to get things done."

Get the idea?

If you are her manager: Often a complainer/whiner really believes that everything is terrible and usually feels that she can't do anything about it. It's important not to agree or disagree when your direct report is going on about how awful things are. Instead, help her to focus on deciding which of her complaints are worth doing something about and which ones aren't. Then, get her focused on learning how to problem-solve. Encourage her to put her energy into changing the things she can and letting go of the things she cannot. If she still whines, as her manager, you can forbid her from complaining by explaining that it is hurting the morale of the rest of the team.

If you are less senior: Because you aren't on this whiny manager's level, it's tempting to avoid her at all costs so you don't have to listen to her. However, most people know intuitively when they are being avoided. Instead, next time she complains, ask her if you can help her come up with a solution. If she dismisses you, tell her that it's been your experience that it feels better to put energy toward solving a problem (if it's actually a real problem) than not doing anything about it.

Someone blames everyone else for everything that goes wrong, or makes excuses for himself without taking personal responsibility.

If you are a peer: Someone's motive for blaming someone else for something he did can be either to avoid responsibility or to avoid being blamed himself. The same goes for making excuses if he's been caught. If your coworker blames you needlessly, politely state the truth about what happened without sounding defensive. If he continues to blame you, repeat the facts about what happened again.

If you are his manager: Ask him to recite the facts, and ask over and over again, "What part did you play in this situation?" People who externalize the reasons for their problems usually do so because they feel insecure. A person who habitually blames or "scapegoats" others may be a bully, an insecure type who tries to boost his own fragile ego by putting other people down. Optimists are rarely bullies, nor do they play the "blame game."

If you are less senior: Because this person can have a direct impact on your career, it's quite important for you to set the facts straight as soon as possible (assuming he's blamed you). If he's blaming one of your coworkers, and you were involved, offer to help your coworker straighten out the facts. Whatever you do, though, don't speak directly to the blaming higher-up until you've cleared it with your colleague.

Occasionally, you may have to work with someone who lacks integrity and refuses to take personal responsibility for anything unless it serves his or her purposes. In this kind of situation, there's not much you can do other than try to expose this individual's ethical deficiencies to those in a position to do something about it.

Someone is overly optimistic all the time, or a Pollyanna.

If you are a peer: This isn't the most terrible thing, but there are times when you need a realistic perspective. When this is the case, ask her to help you analyze the downside or risk of a situation and/or remind her of the reality of the situation.

If you are her manager: Decide whether your employee is too optimistic because she's fearful of expressing her opinion or of coming across as negative. Be sensitive to her feelings and encourage her to speak her mind. Reassure her that you value her experience and her opinions, even when they aren't positive. Share any sobering details of a situation where there could be a negative outcome, and ask her to prepare herself for this possible outcome and recognize the reality of the situation.

If you are less senior: It's uplifting to work with an extremely positive senior employee unless he is denying or avoiding what's real by pretending everything is just spiffy. If he is exceedingly optimistic about a specific situation that you feel doesn't merit this assessment, it's your responsibility to inform him of the facts. You can still do this in an upbeat manner.

ASSESS YOUR OPTIMISM

Answer the following questions to help you assess whether or not you are generally optimistic, and to what degree. For each statement below, respond in the way that best describes you. Record your immediate impression. Use the following scale:

5 = Almost always
4 = Most of the time
3 = Usually
2 = Sometimes
1 = Almost never

___ 1. I face challenges with a sense of control.
___ 2. I try to use positive language in my communications with other people.
___ 3. I don't let anxiety I may feel dominate my behavior.
___ 4. My friends and coworkers would definitely describe me as optimistic.
___ 5. I don't panic when something bad happens to me or the people I love because I always see the upside as well.
___ 6. I'm usually the person at work who tries to keep morale up.
___ 7. I focus my energy on positive ideas and thoughts.
___ 8. I believe in the saying "Don't cry over spilled milk."
___ 9. When I apply for a job, enter a contest, or involve myself in other competitive situations, I expect to do well.
___ 10. When I detect something abnormal about my health, I immediately assume I'll be just fine.
___ 11. When I go to a movie that has received mixed reviews, I assume that I will enjoy it, regardless of the negative reviews.
___ 12. My best friend leaves an urgent message on my cell phone. I automatically think he has good news.
___ 13. I don't let my doubts or fears get in the way of my goals.

___ 14. I don't let my mistakes discourage me from trying again.

___ 15. I believe that my expectations of myself are responsible for my success.

___ 16. I don't understand why someone wouldn't try to be optimistic at all times.

SCORE KEY

Add up the numbers that you entered for each question. If you scored:

16 to 28—You really are quite pessimistic most of the time. Not only will your attitude affect your success in life, but other people really have trouble dealing with you because of your negative outlook. Can you think about the reasons why you are so deeply pessimistic? As a child, was there a significant adult in your life who was pessimistic? Has your lack of confidence or bad life experiences caused you to lose your optimism? Whatever the reason for your negativity, if you don't work on brightening up your attitude, you'll most likely continue on a downward spiral that can do serious damage to both your personal and professional relationships—and make you miserable in the process!

29 to 41—You've allowed life to drag you down to a point where your automatic response to most situations is negative. Making a conscious decision to become more optimistic is the first step toward climbing out of your negative rut. Next time something bad happens to you, instead of instantly reacting negatively, step back and think of any possibly hopeful or positive aspects of the situation first. Case in point: Rich's house burned down last winter because of a clogged chimney flue. He and his wife and daughter were unhurt in the fire, and that's all he focused on until he recovered from the shock of what happened. True, a terrible thing had happened, but Rich knew that in order to move forward, he and his family had to focus on their *well-being,* and *not* on the loss of all of their material belongings.

42 to 54—You tend to waver between optimism and pessimism, and may even have convinced yourself that you are more optimistic than you really are. As with most people, specific incidents, situations, and people probably trigger your attacks of pessimism. Think about your life and work. Try to

identify the things that trigger pessimistic thoughts in you. For each one, try to figure out why this is true. Using this practical technique can help put you on the road to Optimism.

55 to 67—You possess a healthy and balanced degree of Optimism and typically rely on it to understand and deal with life's trials. Friends, family, coworkers, and clients generally think of you as an optimistic person and rely on you to help them view the world in a positive yet realistic light.

68 to 80—You are the ultimate optimist. Nothing ever seems to dampen your constantly upbeat disposition. Take care, though, as you may be a Pollyanna who uses optimism as a protective cover to avoid dealing head-on with unpleasant people or situations. If you scored on the high end of this scale, stop and think *honestly* about whether you're genuinely optimistic or you merely use overly positive thinking as a means of denying reality.

If your score fell between 55 and 80 and you sincerely believe that you generally make a real effort to be an optimist *or* you simply don't have to work hard at it, lucky you! As you read earlier in this chapter, you probably are happier, healthier, and more successful than the average person. Just be certain that you aren't walking through life in complete denial about reality. If you are confident that being a "cockeyed optimist" is not a problem for you, but you could use some tips on dealing with chronic naysayers, doom-and-gloom specialists, or Pollyannas, reread the section of this chapter on page 192.

If you scored between 16 and 41, or you simply know in your gut that you need to build up your Optimism and related Keys, read on!

Is Your Outlook Too Negative? Complete This Assessment

If you have seriously pessimistic tendencies, your negative thinking may have become such an ingrained habit that you may not even be aware of when you're doing it. Unfortunately, it doesn't take long to gain a reputation as a Pessimistic Priscilla or Paul. Answering the following questions can help you to detect a negative pattern to your behavior that may need to be changed.

1. Think of a recent situation at work that was negative. Recall the details as best you can. Do you remember how this situation made you feel? How did you communicate to others when relating the situation to them?

Rose just read an e-mail from her boss announcing that because of ongoing cost-cutting measures, the annual sales conference will be reduced from a week in Hawaii to a long weekend in Florida. When Rose read the e-mail, she grumbled under her breath, "It figures. All this company does is lower morale." Rose lost sight of the fact that the conference *could have been canceled but wasn't,* and that as a sales manager she should be thinking of herself as an extension of "this company." Unfortunately, Luis was walking by Rose's office and asked her if everything was OK. Without thinking of the implications of her negativity, Rose made a sarcastic remark about the change in plans for the conference. Within the next two hours, the entire department was gossiping about the unfairness of the company. Had Rose presented management's decision in an upbeat manner, the rumor mill might not have swirled so unfavorably.

Now, think of a similar situation or incident that may have occurred in *your* job or workplace, in which you or someone else used an unnecessarily negative spin that resulted in negative consequences.

_____

_____

_____

_____

2. Think about the situation you described above. How could you (or the person responsible for the negative spin) have put a positive spin on the situation?

_____

_____

3. Remember Scott Ventrella's premise that pessimism can be sporadic? Let's assume this is the case for you. What specific situations tend to push you into a pessimistic tailspin? George finds it very difficult to stay positive whenever his manager attempts to give him constructive feedback. At even a gentle hint of criticism from his boss, George's lack of confidence kicks in and he complains

and mopes for days afterward. Everyone in George's department is aware of his post–performance review funks, and his coworkers have learned to steer clear of him until the cloud has lifted.

Now, write down the drivers that turn *you* into a pessimist.

_____

_____

4. What are some specific, realistic steps you can take to prevent this scenario from happening in the future?

_____

_____

_____

If you found it difficult to answer these questions, particularly question 3, read on for some tips on how to develop a more upbeat attitude toward work and life.

TIPS AND TECHNIQUES FOR IMPROVING YOUR OPTIMISM

Here is a list of things you can do to begin to change your negative reactions to "bad" or difficult circumstances. Check off the ones that you're willing to try in the immediate future.

_____ If you don't exercise regularly, start! Even a brief walk around the block will do wonders for lifting your spirits, not to mention your waistline and your overall physical and mental health.

_____ Smile more often. Pessimistic people tend to frown. As you've probably heard, it takes many more facial muscles to frown than to smile.

_____ Dump your negative friends and avoid negative coworkers as much as you're reasonably able to. As the adage goes, "Misery loves company."

_____ Read about Key #6: Humor. People who use Humor often and effectively tend to be either optimists or optimistic pessimists!

_____ Eat healthy foods and get enough sleep. Healthy people are energetic, alert, and have more positive attitudes than those who don't take good care of themselves.

_____ Take the focus in your life away from you and put it on others. Read about Key #4: Empathy and Key #10: Respect to get a perspective on how to actually do this. Self-involved people tend to be negative because they aren't reaping the rewards of giving to others.

_____ Find a role model or coach who can help you learn to become more optimistic. Optimism is a habit. The more optimistic you are, the more optimistic you become.

_____ When you're feeling negative, don't suppress your thoughts. Instead, analyze them right away. Why do you feel the way you do about the situation? Is your outlook realistic? What can you do to change your perspective in a positive way? Doing this analysis may help you to understand the root of your pessimism and to move on more quickly.

_____ After you have experienced a disappointment or tough situation, do something pleasurable as soon as you can. Doing so will help you to begin feeling positive again.

_____ We all experience setbacks. Most of us recover from them, too. When a bad thing happens to you, keep reminding yourself that you will grow stronger from it and that you will heal and cope.

_____ Imagine your life as if everything were perfect. No one's life is ever perfect, of course, but if yours were, what would it look like? Think about your personal and professional relationships, the kind of work you do, where you live, your lifestyle, your activities and hobbies, your physical, spiritual, and psychological state, etc. Write it all down. Which aspects can you commit to improving?

_____ Stop using negative language and substitute positive words such as "when" instead of "if," "can" instead of "can't," and "and" instead of "but." If you practice this regularly, it will become a habit.

_____ Read about Key #1: Confidence. Pessimistic people tend to suffer from low confidence. Overall, the more confident in life you are, the more optimistic you'll be.

One of the hallmarks of a pessimist is that he or she often plays the role of victim. Constantly playing the victim can lead to what Martin Seligman calls "learned helplessness." If you tend to externalize your problems, always blaming them on other people or circumstances, you avoid taking personal responsibility for your life. Naturally, things do happen in life that are beyond your control, but you *can* control most things that take place in your life. Deciding not to react like a victim can be a great leap toward becoming an optimist.

Maxine likes to joke about the fact that she is a poster girl for the Department of Unemployment—in the last three years she's been laid off four times in a row. Maxine truly has legitimate reasons for each layoff and works hard at practicing her responses for the inevitable interview question, "Why have you had so many jobs in three years?" Maxine could easily become a victim, yet anyone who knows her can honestly say that she has never bad-mouthed a former employer, that she recognizes and appreciates the valuable aspects of each of her previous jobs, and that she always manages to see the humorous side of her amazing run of bad luck.

Wallace Wilkins, vice president of the Mediation Training Institute in Seattle, recommends a strategy for delaying negative reactions. He calls it "strategic procrastination." Wilkins advises intentionally "procrastinating" your judgment about an unwanted event that has taken place until you get evidence about its future benefits. He uses Alicia as an example. Alicia was diagnosed with a life-threatening disease and initially became angry and depressed. She then decided to stop making assumptions about her illness and to take control of her life. She rekindled several friendships, delegated household responsibilities to her husband and children, requested a lateral transfer within her company, and went to graduate school. Alicia attributes her early negative moods to making up her mind prematurely and now views her disease as a catalyst for change and every challenge as something that holds future benefits.

Are You a Cockeyed Optimist?

Have you been accused of being someone whose glass is overflowing all the time? While you may truly feel this way about yourself and your life, your attitude could be perceived by others as unrealistic. A lack of realism is bothersome to people who want your decisions and action to stem from the truth. Be careful of being too automatic in your positive responses. Next time you feel the urge to say something overly positive, take a deep breath, pause, and ask about the specific details. Admit that the negative aspects are troublesome, offer to help solve the problem, and then go ahead and say something positive. Balancing your overly positive reactions with acknowledgment of the negative elements is a much more palatable approach for your coworkers to handle.

CREATE AN ACTION PLAN TO CURB YOUR PESSIMISM

Rachel has frequently been told by her husband and friends that she's a pessimist and that her constant negativity can be unpleasant to be around. Last week, during her performance appraisal, Rachel's boss told her that he would like her to work on being more positive with her staff and on trying to be more upbeat when things go wrong. Unfortunately, Rachel's boss didn't coach her on how to actually accomplish these goals. Secretly, Rachel fears that at age forty-five it may be hard for her to change her pessimistic ways, but she has decided that her perpetually gloomy attitude is hurting too many relationships that are important to her. Since Rachel is someone who needs to plan things before doing them, she has decided to develop an action plan for becoming more optimistic. Here is Rachel's action plan:

My goal: I am going to respond in a positive manner to everything negative that happens, even if I don't feel this way inside.

MY SHORT-TERM OBJECTIVES/ACTIVITIES:

1. I am going to sit down and make a list of all the good things in my life, including some of the great people I work with, my job, my employer, my husband and children, and myself.
2. Whenever possible, I am going to avoid close contact with anyone who is constantly negative. There are a few people in my life whom I can't avoid (like my mother), so when they say something pessimistic, I am going to get into the

habit of responding positively. For example, the other day my mother commented that I should be paid more in my job. I agreed with her. What I could have said instead was, "Oh, Mom, of course I feel like I should be making more money. Who doesn't feel this way? But I happen to be lucky. What's really important is that I enjoy my job and the people I work with."

MY MEDIUM-TERM OBJECTIVE/ACTIVITY:

1. I actually saw a course in the Learning Annex catalog on learning how to become an optimist! I am going to sign up and take it in the fall.

MY LONG-TERM OBJECTIVE/ACTIVITY:

1. I want to be known by everyone I know as an optimistic person. I am going to find a coach who is a role model and work with him or her specifically on improving my optimism. In six months to a year from now, I will share what I'm doing with important people in my life such as my husband, children, mother (!), boss, and some colleagues whom I trust. I will ask them to help me with my development plan by telling me when I'm less than optimistic in my outlook and comments.

Now, fill out your own action plan, keeping it simple, just like Rachel did.

My goal:

_____

_____

_____

My short-term objectives/activities:

_____

_____

By when: _____

My medium-term objectives/activities:

_____

_____

_____

By when: _____

My long-term objectives/activities:

_____

_____

_____

By when: _____

Optimistic thinking requires selective focus and the ability to recognize, accept, and make an effort to overcome obstacles. If people are among the obstacles you face, learning how to communicate effectively with them is crucial. Being able to "move on" instead of dwelling on or magnifying the negative aspects of life is the mark of a true optimist.

This quote, attributed to the great American inventor Thomas Edison, one of the most famous optimists of all time, says it all: "Results? Why I have gotten a lot of results! If I find ten thousand ways something won't work, I haven't failed. I am not discouraged, because every wrong attempt discarded is another step forward. Just because something doesn't do what you planned it to do doesn't mean it's useless."

Key #9:
Perseverance

Our greatest glory is not in never failing but in rising up every time we fail.
—RALPH WALDO EMERSON

Perseverance is the purposeful, ongoing pursuit of goals and dreams along with the ability to finish what we begin. Perseverance involves setting goals, planning, executing your plan, and taking small steps *and* large leaps with a concentrated focus toward changing or achieving something. To persevere requires patience, tenacity, and endurance—until you complete the task, reach your goal, or master a skill—despite obstacles, adversity, or even suffering. Perseverance can be thought of as an insurance policy for success. But Perseverance isn't a Key to be used just for monumental accomplishments or tough times. It's also important to persevere when things are going well. While smelling the roses is important, success can make us complacent, even lazy.

People who know how to persevere feel in control of their lives. They are usually optimistic self-starters who have a high tolerance for frustration, have high expectations, and believe that meaning and ful-fillment are always within their reach.

It goes without saying that Perseverance is a good trait to possess at work. So much of work is focused on getting things done, reaching goals, starting and finishing projects, and meeting business objectives. Organizational effectiveness depends upon developing talent, team-work, innovation, productivity, making sales, generating revenue, achieving profitability, creating efficiency, upholding quality, and earning customer loyalty. But even the most well-oiled machines can have a wrench thrown into the works from day to day, and one must overcome these obstacles in order to meet his or her goals.

None of this can be achieved without the effort and Perseverance of employees, both as individuals and together. This is truer now, in our era of immediacy and speedy change, than ever before. If you are someone who tends to give up easily, in your work or in your relationships, you may find yourself in trouble and eventually could even be in danger of losing your job. It's equally troublesome if you work with someone who doesn't persevere, because their inaction creates roadblocks for your effort to get things done.

It's easy to let the constraints of the workplace interfere with one's ability to persevere. If, for example, you work in an environment where layoffs and restructuring keep occurring, it's hard enough to simply try to hang on. Everyone is affected differently by change and turmoil. If half the people on your team or in your department aren't working hard and getting things done, the pressure on you increases and you may experience a slump in your own motivation and morale. Despite this challenge, your success will be greater and survival less painful if you make a conscious effort to persevere, even when others aren't doing so. Mark has survived three rounds of layoffs in his division. While he misses his friends who have been let go, he sees the situation as an opportunity to learn new skills and help the company move back "into the black." He works hard despite a serious lack of resources, and his effort and positive attitude do not go unnoticed by senior management.

History is filled with many examples of famous politicians, inventors, artists, businesspeople, and other high-profile individuals who persevered until they reached their goals and fulfilled their dreams. Abraham Lincoln failed in business twice, had a nervous breakdown, was defeated eight times for public office including that of vice president, and lost his sweetheart to illness when he was twenty-six years old. Despite all these events, he kept on keeping on, and eventually he was elected president of the United States at age fifty-one!

Cartoonist Charles Schulz flunked classes throughout his school years, never asked a girl out in high school, and had no friends; his drawing, the only thing he could do easily, was rejected by Walt Disney Studios. He created an autobiographical cartoon character called Charlie Brown, who became the most famous cartoon character ever!

These stories are inspiring because they convey an important message: "If you persevere, you will succeed."

Excessive perseverance, on the other hand, can have a downside. Relentless people who mercilessly forge ahead can be obsessive and tyrannical, lacking Empathy, Flexibility, and Self-awareness. Eileen is a good example. As a project manager, Eileen is responsible for developing the objectives and timelines for major projects at her organization and for monitoring their progress. Her skills are ideally suited for this job except for one thing—in her zeal to complete tasks under budget and on deadline, Eileen inevitably ends up stomping all over her project team. She is so task oriented that many times she forgets to ask for or listen to the input of team members—and drives them to the breaking point in order to show "her" expertise and efficiency.

POINTERS FOR WORKING WITH PEOPLE WHO LACK PERSEVERANCE

What happens when you have to work with someone who doesn't seem to carry her share of the load or who gives up easily? It can be very frustrating to work with this kind of person on a project or toward a common purpose. Here are some suggestions for motivating a colleague who tends to give up too easily or quit when the going gets tough or "boring."

Someone continually misses his deadlines, causing you to miss your deadlines.

If you are a peer: Ask if you can meet with him to discuss how you can both meet your deadlines. In your meeting, probe to find out whether he's missing deadlines because he's apathetic or because he's dependent on other people for information as well. Maybe he's overworked

RELATED KEYS 🔑━━

Key #9: Perseverance

🔑━ **Curiosity** will motivate you to persevere. How? Curiosity is what opens your eyes to opportunity and possibilities through exploration, learning, and understanding.

🔑━ **Optimism** provides the "rose-colored glasses" to peer through in order to believe in yourself and your situation, especially when the going gets rough.

🔑━ **Confidence** is what keeps you on track to believe in yourself and your abilities no matter what.

🔑━ **Decisiveness.** All the elements of Perseverance—such as setting goals, creating a plan, and taking action—require dozens of decisions.

🔑━ **Flexibility** is necessary because, as the non–pet lover's saying goes, "There's more than one way to skin a cat."

🔑━ **Humor** is a Key that supports every one of the other ten Keys, including Perseverance. If you're not able to laugh at yourself and life's odd situations, you won't be able to persevere, especially during tough times.

🔑━ **Self-awareness.** Without knowing what your strengths and weaknesses are, it is impossible to persevere successfully.

or isn't prioritizing this work as important. Before pointing an accusatory finger, it's important to discover what the underlying reason for his tardiness may be. Tell your colleague that his lateness is creating the "domino effect," causing you to be late with your report to your boss. Tell him that you'd like to work it out together and avoid getting anyone else involved, and stress how important this is to you and your reputation. *Do not try to handle this problem in an e-mail; it should be done in a face-to-face meeting.* Document your conversation and keep your notes in a file, in case you need to bring the situation to a manager. If the situation doesn't change, have one more meeting with your colleague before approaching your boss.

If you are his manager: Your approach with him should be similar to the one you'd take as his peer. First, it's important to try to understand the real reasons for his continual tardiness with deadlines. Perhaps there is something you can do to support him as his manager that he's been unable to do by himself, such as prod people who aren't giving him information on a timely basis. Maybe he's not familiar with how to maneuver through the organization or with shortcuts for using technology. Whatever it is, remember that most people don't like to admit that they don't know how to do something—especially to their boss—so your questioning should be diplomatic yet specific.

If you are less senior: Perhaps this person isn't aware of the domino effect his tardiness is having on you and your coworkers? Logically, you might assume he realizes the implications of his actions, but it's really up to you to bring this to his attention. Even if he has bad work habits, presumably he's interested in meeting the organization's business objectives. When you approach him to discuss his missed deadlines, be careful not to point fingers at him. Instead, focus on improving business results.

Someone on your project team doesn't lift a finger unless she absolutely has to.

If you are a peer on her team: First, try to engage your colleague in a discussion about her role on the team to determine her attitude, how invested she is, and whether or not she enjoys her specific role. If you get the sense that she's apathetic or has a bad attitude, it's best to sit down with the team leader and share your observations about the nonworking person. Try very hard to discuss actions and results rather than personality or unsubstantiated gossip.

If you're the team leader: Hold a special meeting to reiterate the expectations you have of the team as a whole and the accountability that each team member has (for example, being respectful of one another, not judging other people's ideas, working hard, each member carrying their share of the load, and being enthusiastic about achieving the team's goals). During this meeting, ask each team member if there are any obstacles or challenges of which you may not be aware. You can even be more direct and pull the person aside and tell her your observations about her contributions (or lack thereof). If the person in question continues to shirk her responsibilities, partner her with someone with whom she must share her progress on a daily basis. This person should not be you but instead someone who is a peer and can be a good role model.

If you are less senior: A successful team means that everyone shares mutual accountability for respecting each other and sharing responsibility. Sometimes individuals have to put aside their individual goals in favor of team goals. There's nothing wrong with expressing this to someone who you don't believe is carrying his or her share. It's intimidating to do this with someone above you, but you can explain it in the context of being on a productive team with a common purpose. At the same time, be sure that you have made the right senior people aware of how much of the load you are carrying and that you've tried to talk to the higher-up who is a slacker.

Someone does appear to be trying hard but falls short in the quality of the work he's doing.

If you are a peer: Ask him if you can coach or mentor him in the area in which he is struggling. If he's offended by your offer, tell him that you've been fortunate to have people in your work life who have helped you and that you'd love to return the favor and help him. As a last resort, if he is closed or defensive about getting help, approach your direct manager and ask for advice.

If you are his manager: Have a performance discussion with him to talk about what's at the core of his difficulties. If he seems to be working hard, his attitude is probably in the right place. Is he missing skills, experience, knowledge, or resources? It's likely to be one of these areas, all which can be remedied with your patience and support and his motivation.

If you are less senior: Oh boy, this situation is sensitive. It's really not your place to involve yourself in a higher-up's lack of performance unless it is really impacting your work tremendously. If it is, it's probably best to talk to your manager about how to handle it. If it's *your* manager, then you'll either have to bite your tongue or approach him carefully if his poor performance is affecting your ability to get things done.

HOW GOOD ARE YOU AT TRYING AND TRYING AGAIN UNTIL YOU SUCCEED?

What if you are the person who lacks Perseverance? If you are, it's likely that your coworkers feel frustrated with you.

ASSESS YOUR PERSEVERANCE

The following self-assessment will help you to determine the degree to which you persevere at work and in your life. Use the following scale:

5 = Almost always
4 = Most of the time
3 = Usually
2 = Sometimes
1 = Almost never

___ 1. I have a clear vision for my life.

___ 2. I take time to plan and prioritize the things I need to accomplish.

___ 3. It's unusual for me not to achieve my goals.

___ 4. I am very skilled at managing distractions and interruptions.

___ 5. I'm able to ignore the naysayer who tries to discourage me from achieving my goals, even if it is someone close to me.

___ 6. I have accomplished things that people consider to be admirable.

___ 7. My energy and "stick-to-itiveness" are two of my greatest strengths.

___ 8. I'm able to bounce back from disappointments quickly.

___ 9. "Quit" is not a word in my vocabulary.

___ 10. I agree wholeheartedly with the statement "Only I can fulfill my dreams."

___ 11. I find it difficult to understand people who don't take charge of their lives.

___ 12. I don't miss deadlines, even if I don't believe in what I'm doing.

___ 13. I possess a very healthy level of emotional and physical stamina.

___ 14. I view obstacles and barriers as challenges.

___ 15. I believe that my expectations of myself are what determine my success.

___ 16. I have a solid support network and role models in my life that I can turn to when times are tough.

SCORE KEY

Add up the numbers that you entered for each question. If you scored:

16 to 28—Your lack of Perseverance can stem from many things. Is your self-confidence low? Do you suffer from fear . . . of failure, success, or something else? Do you believe that your lack of knowledge, education, or experience is preventing you from achieving goals? Or do you simply not allow yourself to have goals or dreams? Whatever the reasons are for your limited Perseverance, it's important that you determine them first so that you can deal with them and stop allowing them to interfere with moving forward.

29 to 41—There have been some times in your life when you've persevered in order to achieve something that was meaningful to you. Unfortunately, this is not the norm. What is preventing you from persevering more consistently? Do you set goals at all? Do you have dreams? Think back to the moments when you pursued something hard and finally attained it. Do you recall how you made it happen and the way it made you feel? Can you think about how to recapture this feeling more frequently?

42 to 54—You're persistent when it really matters, but usually only when it matters to you personally. You may even believe that you are more goal-oriented and hardworking than you really are. Inconsistent behavior is very difficult for other people to deal with; if your score fell here, you could be frustrating others with your contradictory behavior. People find it difficult to know when they can count on you to pull your weight.

55 to 67—You do many of the things that a determined and persistent person does: visualize what you want, set goals, plan, follow through, make decisions, and achieve. At times, your energy level and sense of urgency in getting things done can wane. You can easily move through life with the amount of Perseverance you currently exhibit; however, you definitely possess the ability to stretch and achieve even more than you do.

68 to 80—You are widely known as a person who can achieve anything you decide to. You are great at visualizing your goals and dreams and doing whatever it takes to make them happen. You even make it look easy to those who don't know how hard you work. Other people seek your advice constantly for inspiration and motivation. Because you are someone who is known for getting things done, be wary of people taking advantage of your Perseverance by dumping their work on you. It's also possible that you can overuse Perseverance at times. Remember that the danger in doing so is that you might step on other people's toes in the interest of achieving whatever it is you are after.

If your score fell between 55 and 80 and you are convinced that you use Perseverance the majority of the time, you may want to concentrate on helping your less persistent colleagues at work to persevere by recommending some of the activities in the next section.

If you scored between 16 and 54, be assured that this is a Key that you can easily learn by using some specific techniques such as goal setting, creating a plan, visualizing success, and making decisions.

TIPS AND TECHNIQUES FOR IMPROVING YOUR PERSEVERANCE

Audit Your Life—What Would You Like to Achieve?

It's critical to have meaningful and significant goals in the areas of your life that are important to you. Goals give you purpose and focus. Read each category below and decide if there is something specific in that area that you'd like to accomplish. You don't need to have goals in every category, just those that are most relevant to you right now. Goals don't need to be major, just relevant and meaningful. The SMART acronym is very helpful to use when writing goals. Here it is:

Specific—Goals must be clear and specific, stating exactly what is expected, when, and how much. When a goal is specific, it is easy to measure your progress toward completing it.

Measurable—A goal is useless if you can't measure it. It's also tough to stay motivated to complete your goals when you have no milestones to indicate your progress.

Attainable—Goals must be realistic and achievable. The best goals require someone to stretch a bit to achieve them, but they aren't extreme. Goals that are set either too high or too low are meaningless.

Relevant—Goals must be germane to the overall situation. If they aren't relevant, why bother setting them?

Time-bound—Goals must have starting points, ending points, and a fixed duration. Committing to deadlines helps to focus your efforts on completing goals on or before the due date.

Last, a goal should be simple; typically, you should be able to describe a goal using one sentence.

Your Work or Career

Do you have a goal or something you aspire to achieve in your work?

Karl's boss is transferring to a different division and has recommended Karl as his replacement. Karl is excited about the potential promotion but realizes that the higher-ups don't know him very well. He's created a plan to network with four significant people who will make the decision about whom to hire. He's updated his résumé and filled out the application on his company's intranet. Karl has also asked his boss to sit down and coach him on how he can get the job.

Write *your* goal here along with the things *you* need to do to make it happen.

_____

_____

_____

_____

Your Family

What family-focused goals do *you* have?

Ralph knows that he doesn't spend enough time with his twelve-year-old daughter, Debbie. She is very feminine and already interested in boys. Ralph has decided to find a common interest that he and Debbie can explore together. He plans to identify three or four different activities that he and Debbie can choose together, and his hope is that when they are alone, he can start to understand what Debbie might want to do regularly with him.

Now, write down a goal *you* would like to pursue with *your* family. What do you need to learn, understand, or do to make it happen?

_____

_____

_____

_____

Your Health

Jodi has gained fifteen pounds over the last year. Disgusted with herself, she vows to do something about it. Deciding to approach this problem logically, Jodi makes an appointment with a nutritionist. She lives near a beach and immediately finds two "walking buddies" to walk with four miles every day. Once she gets the nutritionist's analysis she will choose an appropriate diet to follow. She plans on being extremely open about what she's doing so that people will ask about her progress, keeping her accountable.

What's *your* health goal? What things do *you* need to do to make it happen?

_____

_____

_____

_____

Your Interests and Hobbies

Is there a specific activity that you really enjoy or haven't tried but would like to get involved with more extensively?

As a beginner tennis player, Roseanne attended tennis camp several years ago and contracted Lyme disease while she was there. She loved tennis, but her experience with the illness intimidated her so much that she never wanted to lift a tennis racket again. Now she's ready to take lessons again and learn the game. She has researched tennis schools in her area and has decided to make tennis her fall activity once the weather cools down. Roseanne is going to spend the summer getting in good physical shape so that she will be in great condition for tennis.

Is there an interest or hobby that *you'd* like to pursue or become more involved with? What things do *you* need to do to make it happen?

_____

_____

_____

Your Finances

Aside from wishing you'd win the lottery, is there something you can improve in the area of finances?

Peter is having a tough time making ends meet. He has watched several TV interviews recently with financial advisers who all seem to agree that people should pay themselves first. When Peter gets his paycheck every two weeks, he has been sitting down and paying all his bills. Now he's decided to open a savings account and put $100 in it first, before paying his bills. He's calculated that if he does this every two weeks, he'll have $2,600 at the end of a year!

What is *your* financial goal? What do *you* need to make it happen?

_____

_____

_____

_____

Your Spirituality

Do you yearn for spiritual or religious fulfillment?

Megan was raised by two atheists and was never exposed to religion. Recently, she has been wondering what it would be like to belong to a formal religious denomination. She has decided to research four different religions to find out if her interest is merely curiosity, or reflects a deeper need. Through Megan's network, she has friends who are involved in each of the four religions she wants to learn about. They are all willing to bring her to their specific houses of worship.

Do *you* have any goals about spirituality or religion? How, specifically, will *you* meet them?

_____

_____

_____

_____

Obviously, it's fruitless to set goals and not act upon them. This is a good opportunity for you to accomplish some things that you may just have been thinking about for a while.

Strengthen Your Skills, Abilities, or Talents

Often, people don't persevere because they believe that they don't possess the skills or competencies that are necessary to succeed. There may be some validity to this, but most people who do persevere don't allow a lack of ability to deter them from their goal. Nevertheless, it's good to constantly be learning new things because it keeps you vibrant and engenders self-confidence. Think of a goal you'd like to achieve. If you completed the assessment on setting goals in different areas of your life, pick one of the goals you just wrote down. Now, identify the skills or competencies you need to accomplish your goal. Do you need to develop or strengthen any of them? Phil works in the information technology department of his company but wants to become a project manager. When he thought about what he needed to do to get hired in this job, he listed the following things:

- I don't handle my time very well. I'd better take a time-management class.
- Project managers are certified with the project-management institute. I'm going to check the Web site and read about what I need to do to start the process.

- The head of project management here at my company barely knows me. I'm going to call him this week and ask if I can have an informational meeting with him. I'd better buy a book on how to handle this kind of meeting.

Success breeds success. The more frequently you decide to accomplish something and actually do so, the easier it becomes to keep setting goals and achieving them. You'll no longer be thought of as someone who doesn't work hard, keep focused, or follow through. Most important, you'll have the confidence to persevere.

Visualization

Actively imagining the results that you would like to have before you do something is a technique that works well to help make something happen. It also can be used to "see" the outcome of the nonsuccesses that you might be fearful could occur. This process, called visualization, involves imagining every one of your senses in the situation you're dealing with. For example, Penny is planning on entering a marathon race. The longest distance she has ever run is five miles. She's terrified that she won't be able to complete the entire twenty-six miles or that she'll finish but come in last in the race. First, she needs to imagine what it would be like if her fears are realized. She closes her eyes and envisions running fourteen miles and then dropping out because of leg cramps. She also hears her husband, her biggest fan, cheering her along the race route. She imagines having a celebration dinner that night with him and, with a delicious cabernet, toasting the fact that she ran fourteen miles! She closes her eyes again and sees herself crossing the finish line in last place. Penny realizes that even if this happened, she would have achieved a goal she would never have imagined. Not so shabby!

Now, *you* try it. Sit quietly and think about one of your goals and how you would picture a successful outcome. What would it look like? What would you feel, taste, hear, or smell?

_____

_____

_____

_____

Setting goals, identifying specific skills and competencies to learn, and using visualization are three simple yet very effective techniques for persevering. Another important thing to do is to find people who believe in you and support you. These people should not be negative or judgmental toward you. Sometimes it's easier to find acquaintances or even strangers who can support you. Kitty is planning on starting a résumé-writing business and has made a concerted effort to eliminate the people in her life who are negative, not only about themselves but about Kitty. Unfortunately, her mother is one of these naysayers. Kitty wants to continue to have a relationship with her so she is working with a coach to help her learn how to respond to her mother when she makes negative comments.

DO YOU OVERUSE PERSEVERANCE?

Julia is ambitious, focused, and driven to achieve increasingly challenging goals. She's been this way her whole life and isn't always aware of how her quest for success affects other people. Her colleagues always appreciate having Julia on their team when large projects or difficult tasks are involved. Julia keeps everyone on deadline and can single-handedly complete any task, with no sweat! Her attention to both the big picture and details is impeccable, and nothing seems to discourage her from her mission.

The downside? Julia expects all her coworkers to expend the same level of talent and energy as she does. If they fall short, Julia becomes abrupt, impatient, and disdainful toward her colleagues. When this happens, she alienates everyone, creating low team morale, which, in turn, stalls productivity.

Ironically, Perseverance—the very Key that is Julia's strength—serves to dampen everyone else's ability to persevere when she overuses it. People who overuse Perseverance are relatively rare. Many of us are driven and focused in one area of our lives, but not in every area, all the time. If you think you have a tendency to be an overly persistent go-getter, be aware of how you treat other people. Does your drive to achieve your goals negatively impact your relationships?

CREATE AN ACTION PLAN

Liz and Amy started a human-resources consulting firm two years ago with a third partner, Kate. Kate was a hard worker but continually offended nearly every prospective client. When her abrasive personality and lack of Empathy drove away their biggest client, Liz and Amy decided to ask Kate to leave the partnership. After a messy lawsuit, and deflated and demotivated, Liz and Amy knew they had to pick up the pieces and forge ahead, but lacked the drive to do so. They decided to write an action plan that would help them with the elements of Perseverance (planning, goal setting, executing the plan, and taking action). Here is Liz and Amy's action plan:

Our goal: We are going to develop $150,000 of new business by the end of next quarter.

OUR SHORT-TERM OBJECTIVE/ACTIVITY IS:

1. Create a small advisory board by inviting seven people whom we respect to a brainstorming session in three weeks. We will set the agenda and ask them for specific input in the areas of our mission, strategy, and marketing plan.

OUR MEDIUM-TERM OBJECTIVE/ACTIVITY IS:

1. Identify the six best tactics that come out of the meeting and implement them in a timely manner. We will each be accountable for three tactics and will write down all the action steps with a timeline for each one.

OUR LONG-TERM OBJECTIVES/ACTIVITIES ARE:

1. Attend two national conferences this fall where we can exhibit and learn about new trends in our field.
2. Develop six new clients by the end of this fiscal year.

Now, fill out *your* own action plan, keeping it simple just like Liz and Amy did.

My goal:

_____
_____
_____

My short-term objectives/activities are:

_____
_____
_____

By when: _____

My medium-term objectives/activities are:

_____
_____
_____

By when: _____

My long-term objectives/activities are:

_____
_____
_____

By when: _____

Perseverance is a Key that is easier to learn and use than some of the other Eleven Keys. At times, we all avoid doing things we don't like. If you *consistently* procrastinate, miss deadlines, quit projects or activities as soon as they become routine or boring to you, or engage in other self-defeating behaviors, you may be an "underachiever." Continually achieving less than you are capable of isn't necessarily a permanent condition. You can turn it around by using some of the techniques in this book. Read about Key #1: Confidence and Key #3: Decisiveness to help you get started.

The inspiring TV movie *Door to Door* (2002) tells the real-life story of Bill Porter, played by actor William H. Macy. Afflicted by cerebral palsy, Porter had trouble walking, talking, and controlling his limbs. Despite his disability, he worked for the Watkins Company as a door-to-door salesman for thirty-eight years, walking ten miles a day, carrying a heavy sample case, and enduring the stares of ignorant and insensitive people. After twenty-four years, Porter was recognized as the top salesperson in his division. His personal philosophy is a watchword for anyone who wants to understand the value of Perseverance and how it works: "Decide what you want out of life; look on the positive side; and never give up until you achieve it."

Key #10:
Respect

*In the final analysis, true justice is not a matter of courts
and law books, but of a commitment in each of us to
liberty and mutual respect.*

—PRESIDENT JIMMY CARTER

The easiest way to describe Respect is to quote the Golden Rule, "Do
unto others as you would have them do unto you." Respect means
considering another person's needs, thoughts, feelings, wishes, and
preferences even when they are different from your own.

Human beings aren't born knowing how to be respectful of each
other. As young children, we learn how to show respect for others
when we ourselves are consistently treated with respect by our parents, siblings, relatives, teachers, and friends. If the significant people
in our lives fail to treat us with kindness and care, we may begin to
suffer from a lack of self-respect that can, in turn, cause us to behave
disrespectfully toward others.

You may find it surprising that we even need to discuss the impor-

---

What's the difference between self-confidence and self-respect? Self-
confidence means having a realistic belief in yourself and your abilities,
while self-respect means having proper regard for yourself as a human being.

tance of showing respect for other people. But in our modern society, taking the time to treat other people with respect has been on the downslide (witness road rage, the inappropriate use of cell phones, people impatiently pushing ahead of others on store lines, and so on), and nowhere is this disturbing trend more apparent than in the workplace.

Most work environments have become more and more "dog-eat-dog," in part because of the miracle of modern technology. Work never shuts down, priorities constantly change, and people are working harder and longer, stressed beyond belief. Spending long hours in a hostile work environment can make it difficult to maintain respect for one's self, and even more difficult to maintain a respectful demeanor toward colleagues.

The Respect Key means many things:

- Having good manners.
- Expressing thanks when someone does something nice for you.
- Keeping your word.
- Being honest.
- Not blaming others when something goes wrong.
- Being kind.
- Listening.
- Behaving professionally, behaving ethically and with integrity.
- Appreciating personal, cultural, and religious differences.

Respect that is driven by fear, awe, submission, or obedience to another person is not healthy and is likely to morph into resentment. On the other hand, respect that is earned or that stems from value, excellence, or quality is authentic and sustainable.

Most organizations have policies in place to protect the rights of their employees in cases of disrespectful workplace behavior, such as sexual harassment and discrimination. They offer training to orient employees to the official guidelines in these areas. More and more companies are implementing "diversity training" programs to teach employees how to accept and appreciate their mutual racial, religious, or ethnic differences. The U.S. government has enacted federal legislation that prohibits discrimination against specific groups of people based on age, disability, and other special characteristics. But, as popular wisdom teaches, you can't legislate behavior or morality. Emotional, psychological, and even physical abuse takes place every day at a workplace near you.

You don't have to exhibit disrespectful behavior yourself to set a bad example—you can simply condone it. Jack is the head of public relations for a giant media company. His agility with the press is unsurpassed, but so is his temper. He has thrown his phone and his chair at employees on several occasions, and his boss, the company president,

---

Respecting Your Colleagues' Time

Today's workplace never shuts down. E-mail and meetings are endless; no matter what your job is, you probably feel as if you have too much responsibility and not enough time to get everything done. Part of managing time well is using the best organizational system; managing paper; accessing information; managing phone and e-mail messages; managing storage, workspace, and desk layout; managing computer organization; and being able to marshal resources (people, money, material, and support) to get things done. The more effectively you can manage your time, the less stressed you'll be and the more you'll accomplish. If you have an inability to do any of these things, you will infringe upon your coworkers' time. Even if it is not intentional on your part, you are demonstrating disrespect.

Respect is the only Key that always works in your favor—you can never be too respectful. Perhaps someone could argue that a person may be too nice or too accepting of others. But Respect will never be mistaken for weakness. The truth is, we need more respectful people to compensate for the scores of nasty, unethical, unprofessional, and rude people populating our offices and other workplaces.

continually turns a blind eye. Jack receives a "slap on the wrist" from human resources for every incident of bad behavior, but the consequences of his atrocious actions—for Jack—are never more severe than that. His employees cower in his presence, and turnover in his department is at nearly 100 percent. What does this say about Jack's boss and his employer? That they condone disrespectful behavior!

A 2002 survey conducted by University of North Carolina professor Christine Pearson found that 775 employees of both genders reported having been targets of "rude, insensitive, discourteous behavior" at the office.

RELATED KEYS ⌀━━▾

Key #10: Respect

⌀━▾ **Confidence** is a close cousin to self-respect. It's hard to respect others if you don't respect yourself; it's hard to respect yourself if others don't treat you with Respect.

⌀━▾ **Optimism** helps you to stay realistic about yourself or your situation, especially when times are tough.

⌀━▾ **Empathy** gives you the ability to understand someone else. The more you understand someone, the more natural it will be for you to respect them.

⌀━▾ **Curiosity** drives you to explore, learn about, and appreciate people, things, cultures, and traditions that are unfamiliar to you.

⌀━▾ **Humor** is a pressure valve that helps alleviate stress and anxiety, two factors that cause people to be disrespectful of others when they wouldn't behave this way under normal conditions.

⌀━▾ **Self-awareness.** If you don't realize that your behavior may be affecting someone else adversely, then you are sadly out of touch with yourself.

POINTERS FOR WORKING WITH PEOPLE WHO LACK RESPECT

HOW DO YOU DEAL WITH BAD BEHAVIOR AT WORK?

Someone bullies you or your coworkers. Bullying is any kind of behavior that is offensive, intentionally hurtful, physically or emotionally abusive, intimidating, malicious, or insulting. A bully can also be someone who uses power or authority inappropriately.

If you are a peer or less senior: Most bullies are deeply insecure individuals who victimize other people who appear to be weak or vulnerable. If you find yourself in a situation where you are being bullied, the first thing to do is remind yourself of this fact: Most bullies back down when their intended victims react to their bullying behavior with assertive resistance. As soon as someone starts to try to bully you, *tell him on the spot* that he is acting like a bully and that you will not tolerate his behavior. *Don't wait until later.* Most people are afraid to confront bullies, but it's your right as an employee, and as a human being, to protest this kind of behavior and to take whatever legal means are at your disposal to put a stop to it. If the bullying behavior keeps happening and you've discussed it with the offending individual several times, it's time to bring the matter to human resources. If the situation doesn't improve, your bullying coworker's boss is your next stop. Sometimes bullies aren't motivated to change their behavior because they aren't given the incentive to do so. If you are unable to get the appropriate support from management, the behavior may continue unchecked. If this happens, you may have to decide whether or not it's worth your staying in your job. You may come to a valid conclusion that your workplace is seriously dysfunctional and that you'd be better off working in a healthier work environment. It's especially tough to handle a bully who is the CEO or president of your organization. There are too many people out there running companies who are bullies and seem to revel in having this reputation, perhaps mistakenly thinking that they can lead by fear and intimidation. Long term, it's not a good idea to tolerate this kind of behavior, even if it's from someone at the helm of your company. If you are getting a lot out of your job and the kind of work you do, it may be worth your while to soldier on and handle the top dog's bullying for a time. However, when it becomes intolerable and he doesn't change, you'll owe it to yourself to move on.

If you are his manager: Any inappropriate behavior or performance issues should be documented. You should have a discussion with your employee about his bad behavior as soon as it occurs. In a way, this issue is easier than most to deal with because you can explain to your employee that bullying is unacceptable behavior. Perhaps your direct report is accustomed to treating people badly in his personal life, so it would be helpful to offer suggestions for ways to behave and communicate differently. Be clear with your employee that continued mistreatment of others is grounds for termination. If you work for an organization that hires outside coaches to help change behavior such as his, this may be an option before termination. Hopefully, he'll get the message and change his behavior before this drastic last step.

Someone behaves unethically or without integrity, such as blatantly lying about things that directly affect you.

If you are a peer: Proceed with caution. This is very sensitive ground. It's important to analyze the implications of being a "whistle-blower" before you even consider taking action. You may want to consult someone knowledgeable and whom you trust—who is *not* an employee at your workplace—to get an objective opinion. If you've thought it through carefully and are willing to try to stop the person in question from behaving unethically, always be sure that you have discussed her unethical actions with her first and documented your conversation. Say that you're uncomfortable with the specific behavior, especially if it affects you directly or requires your involvement. If she denies it or brushes you off and you still feel *even a little* uncomfortable, you should seriously consider confiding in someone you trust outside your organization and solicit some practical advice. The bottom line in a situation like this is that if someone else's unethical behavior is in conflict with your moral values, it will not be easy to swallow for long and could reflect poorly on your own reputation. And one more thing—if you're planning to make an allegation of unethical or illegal behavior against a colleague, it is *essential* that you have *concrete* proof with which to back your argument. Human resources should always be involved even if that department is generally perceived not to have much power in your company.

If you are her manager: Again, be sure that you have plenty of evidence that she has acted unethically or without integrity. Have a confidential meeting with her and ask her about the specific situation without accusing her of lying, cheating, stealing, or whatever behavior you suspect. If she denies any wrongdoing, ask her for evidence to substantiate her story. If she is unable to provide this or admits her guilt, tell her that you must involve human resources who may also consult legal counsel. Depending on the severity of her actions, you may either give her a written warning or have to terminate her.

If you are less senior: Read the advice given above for someone who is a peer, and immediately inform your manager of the situation. If your manager is the unethical senior person in question, go to human resources right away.

Someone is rude, has no manners, and is inconsiderate or impolite.

If you are a peer: It's helpful to first observe whether he behaves this way with everyone or with just a certain few people. Then, sit down with him and explain why you're uncomfortable with his rude behavior. The workplace is not a children's sandbox (although it may seem that way at times). He might shrug it off or tell you to lighten up, but be persistent. Sometimes, the only tactic that works with a rude person is to continually point out his rude behavior every time he does it. Here is an example: Martha is friendly to everyone in her department except Scott, whom she just doesn't like. When she invites everyone else to join her for lunch, she blatantly ignores Scott. In department meetings, Martha makes faces when Scott is talking. Her friend Mark, feeling more and more uncomfortable with Martha's rude behavior, decided one day to go to Martha's cube and talk with her about it. He explained that her outward rudeness toward Scott made him terribly uncomfortable. Martha behaved defensively at first but later came back to Mark and told him that, while she still didn't care for Scott, she was going to be more courteous to him. It would have been easier for Mark to complain to his coworkers about Martha behind her back, but he had the courage to go to her directly, and it paid off.

If you are his manager: While you may feel like a babysitter at times, part of your management responsibilities involve pointing out your employee's bad behavior to him. When you have this kind of discussion, focus on how his actual behavior affects his coworkers, rather than on his personality. Take the earlier example of Martha being rude to Scott in front of everyone else. As Martha's manager, you'd explain that her behavior doesn't help teamwork, instead of pointing out how rude she is.

If you are less senior: One of your rights as an employee is to be respected by your colleagues, no matter who they are. If a senior person is rude or ill-mannered toward you, don't let him get away with it. Take a deep breath and address it with him as soon as it happens, alone and in private. Pull him aside into a conference room or visit him in his office. Pointing out your boss's bad manners in public is a recipe for disaster. For example, say, "Joe, I would really appreciate it if you would use the word 'please' when you ask me to do something, instead of barking orders at me. Thank you."

Someone ignores, harasses, or blames you for mistakes that aren't yours, or otherwise makes your life miserable.

If you are a peer or less senior: Think carefully about whether the bad behavior is personally directed toward just you, or whether this person behaves this way with many people. Talk to one or two people who know both of you, and whom you can trust. Solicit their honest and confidential opinion regarding this person's behavior toward you. If you decide that it's personal, try to understand what the person's motive is. Does she dislike you because you belong to a specific group that she doesn't like? Is she threatened by you, the position you hold, or the work that you do? Did something happen between the two of you in the past that may have caused her to dislike you? If you've thought it through and still are unable to understand what is motivating her behavior, it's time to sit down with her.

First, decide what your goal is. Do you want to simply stop her bad behavior toward you? Do you want to develop a relationship with her, too? Ask for a meeting in a quiet place, where no one else can hear your conversation. Say that you feel that she does not treat you with courtesy or dignity, and that you'd like to understand why. If she shuts down or gets defensive or abusive, end the meeting. Tell her that you'd like to reschedule the meeting when she is ready to stop behaving in an emotional or abusive manner. Most people will want to retreat and not broach the subject again. Avoid doing this. A good rule of thumb for dealing with *all* disrespectful people: Be assertive. If you have another meeting and she still doesn't listen, tell her that you're not willing to work with her under these conditions and that you must talk to human resources. Involve your manager as well (unless she *is* your manager). Above all, do not back down. You should not have to deal with disrespectful or abusive behavior.

If you are her manager: It's pretty unlikely that your employee is treating you this way. However, if she is treating her coworkers badly and they have complained to you, you must intervene as soon as possible. You'll need to be very clear about what the facts are and ask all employees involved to share their perspectives about what has transpired. If your employee *is* guilty of harassment or "scapegoating," this is a serious matter that should be "nipped in the bud."

What if you aren't as respectful as you could be? Unfortunately, you may not possess enough of the Key Self-awareness to realize this about yourself. To find out, answer these assessment questions as honestly as you can.

ASSESS YOUR RESPECT

The following self-assessment will help you to determine how respectful you are. When answering the questions, use the following scale:

5 = Almost always
4 = Most of the time
3 = Usually
2 = Sometimes
1 = Almost never

___ 1. I try to live by the Golden Rule.

___ 2. "Please," "thank you," "excuse me," and "you're welcome" are words that come naturally to me in my relationships and interactions with others.

___ 3. I believe in doing what I say I am going to do and always try to keep my commitments. If I am unable to do so, I always make an effort to contact the other person immediately to apologize and explain.

___ 4. My friends and family would characterize me as a kind and caring person.

___ 5. I can count the number of times on one hand that I've been rude to people at work.

___ 6. I avoid telling people what to do or what they "should" or "need" to do.

___ 7. I make a real effort to try to understand other people's beliefs, values, and needs.

___ 8. I'm appalled by the apparent lack of ethics and integrity in corporate America.

___ 9. I believe that violence is never a valid conflict-resolution tool.

___ 10. Having a reputation as a professional, courteous, and sensitive person is very important to me.

___ 11. When I am forced to deal with a colleague who is disrespectful, I am very careful not to behave in the same way.

___ 12. I can't recall the last time I gossiped about, insulted, or put down someone at work.

___ 13. I am concerned that there is a growing epidemic of rudeness in America today.

___ 14. I try to compliment or do something nice for someone every day.

___ 15. I don't agree with the childhood chant, "Sticks and stones may break my bones, but words will never hurt me." I believe that words can be used as weapons and can cause deep wounds.

___ 16. I try to be very respectful of others, even when I'm under a great deal of pressure.

SCORE KEY

Add up the numbers that you entered for each question. If you scored:

16 to 28—You are chronically rude and possibly even abusive to your coworkers. Stop and think about why you behave this way. Are you in a position of authority? Do you feel stressed out all the time? Do you get some short-term pleasure out of ridiculing others or hurting their feelings? Did you grow up in a physically or emotionally abusive household? Regardless of the reason for your bad behavior, it's time for you to take a good look at your hurtful actions and learn what being respectful to others really means, and why it's important at work and in life. Until you start to change your behavior, you can be sure of one thing—you are not well thought of or respected by your coworkers. Is this what you really want?

29 to 41—You often treat people with a lack of respect. Are you intolerant of people who are different from you? If so, why do you think this is? Did you grow up in a household where intolerant attitudes were the norm? Do certain people just "push your buttons," and you're not even sure why? Whatever you do that's hurtful or unkind to other people, it's important for you to figure out what benefit you get from behaving this way, and whether it's really worth it. People don't respond positively to disrespectful behavior, and chances are that your coworkers or clients—and possibly some of the people in your personal life—are a bit wary of you. If you care enough to be reading this section, then it's possible that you are ready to make some positive changes.

42 to 54—It's time to look in the mirror and make some serious changes. You have moments when you are a kind, sensitive, and courteous person and times when you are rude or inconsiderate toward or embarrass others. This kind of erratic behavior can be very disconcerting to other people.

It's hard for your coworkers to trust you because they never know which side they are going to witness. Remember that there is *never* a good excuse for disrespectful behavior.

55 to 67—Overall, you are respectful to everyone who crosses your path. You might crack a little under pressure, but don't we all, at times? You deserve kudos for feeling and behaving respectfully toward your colleagues most of the time. Try to work on modifying your reactions to stress, and think about how the ways in which you handle stress may impact your behavior toward others.

68 to 80—You are impressive! People enjoy working with you because you have a smile or kind word for everyone and are a model of integrity. You treat other people exactly the way you'd like to be treated—with dignity, civility, and courtesy. You are extremely uncomfortable around people who ridicule, embarrass, or hurt others because this kind of behavior goes totally against your grain.

If you scored between 55 and 80, congratulations are in order! As someone who displays respectful behavior most of the time, you may struggle with how to deal effectively with people who don't. If so, keep reading for some practical ideas for easing your discomfort.

If you scored between 16 and 54, you have some work to do. Respect is a Key that isn't easy to learn because your disrespectful behavior is either habitual or possibly even ingrained in your personality. You may not intentionally set out to offend or cause distress for anyone, but your attitude or misinterpretation of the signals you get from others may lead you to behave this way. You will have to change your attitude before you can change your behavior. Read on to learn how.

Are You Disrespectful Toward Others? Complete This Assessment

Change Your Attitude

It's well known that attitude drives behavior. For example, if you feel distaste or anger toward a person who belongs to a specific group, you may (even subconsciously) behave poorly toward everyone you interact with who belongs to the same group.

Recognizing, accepting, and appreciating a colleague's differences is something that may not come easily to you. This is especially true if you've had negative or awkward experiences with someone who has certain traits or characteristics that make you uncomfortable. Matt manages five people. Kurt, one of his direct reports, is always missing deadlines. Instead of sitting down with Kurt to help him learn how to get his work done on time, Matt yells at him. What Matt doesn't know about Kurt is that he suffers from dyslexia *and* attention deficit disorder. Kurt is too embarrassed to fill Matt in, and their relationship is deteriorating rapidly.

Think about a coworker or client whose knack for pushing your buttons often results in your saying rude or disrespectful things to this individual. This exercise is for your eyes only. Write the name of the person or the relationship to you at work. Then think of possible reasons why you aren't as courteous or sensitive to him or her as you should be, and write them down, too.

_____

_____

_____

What can you do to change your behavior toward this person?

_____

_____

_____

Do a "Respect Checkup" on Yourself

You read the elements of the Respect Key at the beginning of this chapter. Even if you need to improve this Key, you may not necessarily be deficient in every area. Take a look at the list again:

- Having good manners. _____
- Expressing thanks. _____
- Keeping your word. _____
- Being honest. _____
- Not blaming others when something goes wrong. _____
- Being kind. _____

- Listening. _____
- Appreciating personal, cultural, and religious differences. _____
- Behaving professionally. _____
- Behaving ethically and with integrity. _____

Think about yourself and about feedback you may have received recently from your boss, clients, or coworkers about your behavior toward other people. Check the items above that you need to work on. Next, review the following tips for developing or improving the things you've decided to change.

TIPS AND TECHNIQUES FOR IMPROVING YOUR LEVEL OF RESPECT

Having good manners—Saying "please," "thank you," and "excuse me" are universal expressions of respect in every language. Most people who habitually use these words and phrases learned how to do so as children. Even if you did learn "the magic words" as a young person, it's easy to forget to use them "in the heat of the moment" as an adult. Since sincerity and nonverbal communication are usually more meaningful than empty words, be aware that if you use the words but don't mean them, don't bother! If you're angry, upset, or stressed out, stop—and then pause before speaking. Use the words "please," "thank you," and "excuse me" as often as you can!

Expressing thanks—You don't get much recognition at work, do you? Well, neither does anyone else. Whether you're a manager or a single contributor, you have coworkers who support and help you to be successful in your job. Thank these people, praise them, and recognize them in ways both big and small. If you reward good work by acknowledging it, you'll be rewarded. The goodwill you spread and the smiles of appreciation you put on the faces of the people around you will benefit your whole work environment. You've probably heard the expression, "What goes around, comes around." Most human beings are motivated by appreciation and positive attention—aren't you?

Keeping your word—Everyone values an individual who follows through on commitments. Most jobs require some degree of collaboration. If the colleagues you depend upon can't depend on you in return, you will have problems. Technology, which has brought us the marvelous capability of instant communication, has also raised the bar on people's expectations of one another at work. Now more than ever, time has become a precious commodity. It can be a challenge to manage the constant barrage of requests for information and assistance that most of us encounter on the job. Saying no diplomatically and negotiating with colleagues are important survival skills that can help you to avoid "painting yourself into a corner" and not fulfilling your obligations. Keeping the lines of communication open with your colleagues will make it easier for you to prioritize your commitments and stay true to your word.

Being honest—It's astounding to have to explain why telling the truth is the only option. This is one of the simple lessons that children usually learn from their parents. When people lie to their coworkers or boss, it's usually because they are concerned about getting caught for something they've done wrong or for not following protocol or direction. Usually, it's a coping mechanism for avoiding punishment or ridicule. Honesty really is "the best policy," because conforming to fact is always appreciated by others.

Not blaming others when something goes wrong—If you manage or supervise other people, you are just as responsible for the results of their work as they are. Why? Because it's your job to train, coach, and motivate your staff so that they can achieve their goals and succeed in their jobs. Being a boss means that "the buck stops" with you. There is never a reason to pin the blame on your employees when things go wrong. If you aren't a manager, you're still accountable for your own errors. All human beings sometimes make mistakes. Faulting others when times are tough is not playing fair.

Karen is in marketing at a software company. She depends on the folks in product development (PD) to provide her with timely updates so that she can create marketing campaigns to promote the new products they create. Quite often, the PD people delay the flow of information, causing Karen to miss her deadlines. Instead of being angry, she decided to invite a representative of PD to her weekly staff meeting to deliver a product update and learn what's happening in marketing. Karen's strategy has paid off. With the PD representative keeping her regularly in the loop, she's always on top of her deadlines.

If, like Karen, you make a conscious effort to be a creative problem-solver instead of pointing fingers, your coworkers will respond in kind and are likely to be more invested in helping you achieve your goals.

Being kind—It's a rare human being who doesn't respond well to kindness. Yet, some people are clueless when it comes to treating others with concern, sympathy, or understanding. People are unkind for a variety of reasons. They may have been victims of unkind or abusive behavior themselves, or were never taught as children how to behave with kindness toward others. They may allow their own agenda or emotions to rule their behavior, or they may be insecure in social situations and use harsh or insensitive behavior to mask their true feelings. Someone who is mean or a bully tends to pick on people who appear weak or frightened. There is absolutely *no excuse*—ever—for mean, nasty, or unkind behavior, whether inside or outside the workplace. If you've forgotten how to be kind, think about who the kindest person is at work, and watch that person in action. You may learn something.

Listening—It doesn't matter how smart or talented you are if you don't relate well to people. Individuals who have trouble relating to other people usually have poor listening skills. If you suspect that this is true for you, turn to Key #4: Empathy, for practical tips on how to be a better listener. Your coworkers or customers know when you're not listening to them. Just as we all value kindness, we all like to be heard.

Behaving professionally—Professionalism means displaying proper business etiquette and protocol. As a professional, you're expected to make each individual you interact with feel important, attended to, and respected. You're also obligated to follow formal as well as informal business guidelines and norms, both those that are specific to your company or employer and those that are simple courtesy or common sense.

All work situations—from sending e-mail, participating in meetings, or walking down the hall to attending company functions or communicating bad news to your employees—require professional behavior. It's easy to identify when someone is behaving unprofessionally. The "why" is sometimes harder to grasp. Often, it's just a matter of a lack of experience or common sense. Suzie was recently promoted. Part of her new responsibilities involves meetings with senior management. Suzie was taken aback when her manager questioned her about her actions at a recent meeting with Dr. Barnes, the company's CEO. Since the meeting had been scheduled for noon, Suzie had decided to "kill two birds with one stone" and brought her lunch. Jeb, Dr. Barnes's assistant, had never mentioned anything about lunch. Suzie honestly didn't understand why her behavior was viewed as unprofessional.

Ann Chadwell Humphries, a consultant who specializes in business etiquette, conducted a survey of the rudest and most annoying behaviors at work. They are:

- **Bad telephone manners**—Curt, unfriendly, impolite, and unhelpful; putting people on hold for a long time and hanging up without saying good-bye.
- **Interruptions**—Breaking into other people's conversations or interrupting someone who is explaining something to you.
- **Lack of appreciation**—Not thanking someone; ignoring someone who has just helped you or whom you've just walked past; never paying compliments for contributions or a job well done.
- **Use of inappropriate language**—Swearing and using unsuitable slang (use your imagination!).
- **Inappropriate business appearance**—Unkempt and sloppy clothing; poor hygiene; wearing overly casual clothes or clothing that is too tight or too baggy; and exposed tattoos and piercings.
- **Not being considerate of other people's time**—Constantly being late for meetings and conference calls; missing deadlines; failing to give colleagues information they need.
- **Public criticism/denial of criticism**—Putting someone down in meetings; blaming someone for something that isn't their fault; critiquing coworkers inappropriately.

Jackie and Tanya are partners in their own start-up gourmet dessert business. Since they can't afford to pay a staff yet, Jackie is responsible for marketing, customer service, and bringing in new accounts; Tanya is in charge of production and packaging. Tanya, the mother of two active teenagers, stays in touch with her children during the day by cell phone. Often, when Jackie is out in the field and needs to reach Tanya, Tanya interrupts their phone conversations to take calls from her kids.

Here's a typical conversation:

Jackie: "Tanya, it's me. I'm in my car, on the way to that meeting with Marilyn Jones at Helping Hands and her board president to talk about supplying desserts for their fund-raiser next month. I just realized that I left the new cheesecake brochure at the office. Would you please fax it to me at Marilyn's office?"

Tanya: "Sure. Do you know where you left it?"

Jackie: "Yes, it's on top of the . . ."

Tanya: "Oops! Wait a minute Jackie—hold on, it's Tucker calling from school. Hold on." (Jackie waits.)

Tanya: "Hi. Sorry, Jackie. Now, what were you saying?"

Jackie: "The cheesecake brochure is on the top of the credenza in the . . ."

Tanya: "Oh my, it's Annie this time . . . hold on . . . just a second."

Jackie pulls into the parking lot at Helping Hands, still waiting for Tanya to get back to her. Now she has a dilemma. While she doesn't want to walk into the meeting with their potential new client unprepared, she obviously doesn't want to be late either. She keeps her cell phone on and hopes that Tanya will call soon. You get the picture.

Appreciating personal, cultural, and religious differences—The American workplace is truly a "melting pot" of different nationalities, ethnic backgrounds, religions, and beliefs. While you may not understand the specific qualities and peculiarities of every person you work with, it's important to learn to accept them. Acceptance means not ignoring, judging, or showing contempt for another person simply on the basis of who they are. It's even better if you make the attempt to comprehend the meaning and significance of someone else's differences. Most people gravitate toward people with similar backgrounds because it makes them feel comfortable and they can speak a certain shorthand. But relating only with people who are like you can create resentment and interfere with teamwork—not to mention make your life a lot less interesting!

Behaving ethically and with integrity—An important part of respect is adhering to the rules or standards of conduct that exist in your workplace. Lying, cheating, and stealing are clearly wrong. Other principles of integrity and ethical work behavior include not trespassing on your coworkers' physical space, adhering to official working hours, and always remembering that you are a representative of your employer. As the news headlines too often remind us, we live in an era of unbridled greed. We are all familiar with the many examples of corporations and individuals who have broken laws, lied, cheated, and stolen from their employees, clients, and stockholders. Even you, or some of your coworkers, may be guilty of having taken office supplies home or of occasionally padding an expense account. While these may seem like relatively petty violations that "everyone does from time to time," they are still unethical.

Now it's time to develop your action plan for working on the elements of Respect that you think you need to improve.

CREATE AN ACTION PLAN

Dawn is a manager at a nonprofit agency that helps to feed the hungry. Dawn is a caring and conscientious person, but she doesn't handle stress well, is very emotional, and tends to burst into tears or yell at the top of her lungs at "the drop of a hat." Unfortunately, Dawn directs her emotional tirades toward her staff members. As a result, Dawn's direct reports tiptoe around her and are afraid to approach her, even when they need help or support. Dawn doesn't mean to hurt anyone's feelings or to offend them, but her emotional outbursts have done a lot of damage to her reputation as a manager and professional. The good news is that Dawn knows her behavior is destructive and has to change, so she's going to create an action plan to help her get a handle on her tendency to become overly emotional when she's feeling tense, pressured, and overwhelmed.

Here is Dawn's action plan:

My goal: I am going to *stop* crying in public and yelling at my employees.

MY SHORT-TERM OBJECTIVES/ACTIVITIES ARE:

1. I am going to research books on anger management and buy a few.
2. Francine is calm and "cool as a cucumber," even when a disaster occurs. I trust her implicitly, so I'm going to ask her to share what she does to stay so unruffled.

MY MEDIUM-TERM OBJECTIVE/ACTIVITY IS:

1. I am going to get referrals from my agency's EAP (Employee Assistance Program) and find a good psychotherapist. I really want to know what it is inside me that's triggering my emotional outbursts.

MY LONG-TERM OBJECTIVE/ACTIVITY IS:

1. I'd like to get to know my employees better so that our mutual trust level increases. I'm going to schedule one-on-one meetings with each of my employees over the next six months, as well as something social, like a breakfast or lunch. I may also arrange a department dinner or picnic.

Now, fill out your own action plan.

My goal:

_____
_____

My short-term objectives/activities:

_____
_____
_____

By when: _____

My medium-term objectives/activities:

_____
_____
_____

By when: _____

My long-term objectives/activities:

_____
_____
_____

By when: _____

If you've ever been the recipient of someone else's disrespectful behavior, or the victim of bullying, harassment, or abuse at work, this next section is for you. Individuals who are chronically disrespectful or abusive fall into the "difficult people" category, about which scores of books have been written. Here are some ideas and tips for working with all kinds of disrespectful coworkers.

Dealing with coworkers or clients who are constantly disrespectful to you, or to someone else, can be extremely stressful. Disrespectful people rarely wake up one morning and say to themselves, "Hmm, today I am going to turn into a kind, sensitive, courteous, and professional person with integrity." The good news is that, even though people addicted to being rude and hurtful toward others don't usually change on their own, it's possible for *you* to motivate them to change their behavior.

Your goal in dealing with the disrespectful individual is not to make him or her go away (although this would be nice) but instead to learn to avoid getting into difficult situations with that person. Impossible you say? Not so! All you need to do to elicit different behavior from a rude or abusive person is to change *your* behavior and approach. That's really what using the Eleven Keys is all about. When working with disrespectful people, it's easiest to ignore or avoid them as best you can—as a short-term tactic. (If your situation has really deteriorated, this may be the only survival tactic you have left.) If you are not in desperate straits and can marshal your inner resources, it's always best to confront the situation head-on, by doing the following:

- Face the person.
- Try to understand him and his agenda.
- Stay calm.
- Maintain your sense of humor.
- Present your concerns and ideas for a solution to him.

Sally worked with Nina for several years. Nina exhibited every disrespectful trait described in this chapter: She never listened, blamed everyone else for anything that went wrong at work, was rude and insensitive to coworkers, and routinely cut ethical corners. Sally couldn't stand the sight of Nina. Then one day (miracle of miracles!), Nina quit. Sally was so happy that she practically danced a jig. But Will, Sally's boss, said to her, "Sally, there will *always* be a Nina." And he's right. Get rid of one bad apple, and there will be another one waiting in the wings! You can count on it. Unfortunately, more often than not, Sally would be the one to quit. The only way to fix a toxic relationship in the office is to take a deep breath and calmly face him or her head-on, with conviction and, most important, with the expectation that it can change for the better.

We all have stories of people who have treated us, or someone we know, poorly at work. The person guilty of the offending behavior may be smart, talented, and competent as can be, but falls short when it comes to the *real* bottom line—the Golden Rule. If we held a contest to rate professional skills in order of value and importance, the ability to treat colleagues, coworkers, and clients with respect would win hands down.

The lyrics from the 1960s classic rock anthem, written by Otis Redding and made famous by the "Queen of Soul," Aretha Franklin, remind us of how we all want—and deserve—to be treated: "*R-E-S-P-E-C-T* . . . All I'm asking is *for a little respect!*"

Key #11:
Self-awareness

Know thyself.

—SOCRATES

Self-awareness may well be the most complex of the Eleven Keys, for two reasons—because of what it involves and because it's more difficult to develop. It involves knowing and understanding aspects of yourself and their relation to other people; the meaning of your appraisals and actions; your wants, intentions, and goals and your attitudes, hopes, and fears. It is the Key that unlocks all the other Keys—it's the master Key, for without Self-awareness, it's nearly impossible to develop a balanced level of any of the other Keys. In other words, Self-awareness is at the core of balancing Confidence, Curiosity, Decisiveness, Empathy, Flexibility, Humor, Intelligence, Optimism, Perseverance, and Respect. However, having a high level of Self-awareness does not guarantee that you will automatically command just the right amount of the other Keys. What complicates the relationship between Self-awareness and the other ten Keys is the need to possess many of the other Keys in order to be self-aware.

This book is about work, both the work we do every day in order to live and provide for ourselves and our families, and the work we do every day to make ourselves and the world we live in better. Balancing each of the Eleven Keys is part of making that work easier by having a well-developed sense of Self-awareness. If the Eleven Keys were arranged in this book organically instead of alphabetically, Self-awareness would come first.

Self-awareness is a sophisticated form of consciousness that enables you to become the object of your own attention by being aware of your perceptions, sensations, attitudes, intentions, and emotions as well as your behaviors and general physical appearance. Self-awareness is fundamental and important to possess because it enables you to regulate yourself by self-monitoring, observing yourself, and changing your thought processes and behaviors.

In his model of Self-awareness, Alain Morin, a professor at Mount Royal College in Canada, explains that the three primary sources of Self-awareness are the social environment, the physical world, and one's self. The social world involves receiving verbal and nonverbal feedback from other people and deciding how relevant it is. Morin explains that we have a tendency to accept unimportant but positive feedback and to reject important but negative self-information. The social environment also presents opportunities to make comparisons between yourself and others, which increases Self-awareness. The physical world provides stimuli that generate Self-awareness, such as cameras, mirrors, recordings of your voice, newspapers, television, movies, and the Internet. It's obvious why looking in the mirror or seeing yourself in a video would give you pause to self-assess, but why movies, television, and the Internet? Because these forms of media provide a variety of views and behaviors that might be different from your own, which could motivate you to reassess your own perspective. The third source of Self-awareness is your own self, which generates self-talk, self-imagery, and mental and physical awareness.

Someone who doesn't possess a high level of Self-awareness may not be able to recognize what his attitudes, feelings, emotions, intentions, and behaviors are or how they are perceived. If he doesn't recognize them, he certainly can't manage them. If he can't manage them, he won't be aware of how they might affect you. If he's not conscious of how you've been affected by his emotions, he isn't going to inspire you to feel confident about working with him.

Clara just started reporting to Darren. Recently, she showed Darren a PowerPoint presentation she had created for an upcoming client meeting. The entire time Clara was showing Darren her presentation, he was frowning, yawning, and fidgeting. Clara left Darren's office very upset. A few hours later, when she had calmed down, she went back into Darren's office and asked him why he didn't like her presentation. Darren was astonished and denied that he disliked her presentation. He said he thought it was great and honestly had no awareness of how he came across to Clara in the meeting. Now Clara feels confused and is hesitant to show Darren any client presentations in the future.

POINTERS FOR WORKING WITH PEOPLE WHO LACK SELF-AWARENESS

What happens when you have to work with someone who doesn't seem at all in touch with who she is and how she comes across to others? Here are ideas for working more easily with someone like this.

Someone constantly behaves rudely or inappropriately toward you or your coworkers and you're quite sure he doesn't realize it.
If you are a peer: The next time he does something that makes you uncomfortable, tell him. Describe exactly what he does and how it

Managing Time Effectively

This is one of the most common developmental needs that American workers share. You may not be able to do much about limited resources at work, technology that never shuts down, and the many external demands that work presents you. What you *can* do is manage yourself and your habits so that you can get your work done and deal more easily with other people who don't seem to manage their time well and affect *your* time. A large part of your ability to do this is Self-awareness.

makes you feel in as much detail as possible. If he acts surprised or confused, explain that you're telling him because you want to help him increase his Self-awareness about his actions and the way they impact you and perhaps others. If you truly believe that he is clueless

RELATED KEYS 🔑⊷

Key #11: Self-awareness

⊷ **Confidence** is what keeps you on track to believe in yourself and your abilities, especially when you receive uncomfortable feedback.

⊷ **Curiosity** will motivate you to learn and understand more about yourself. It also will enable you to be curious about how you affect others.

⊷ **Decisiveness.** It doesn't matter how much Self-awareness you have if you don't decide to change your behavior, attitudes, and emotions.

⊷ **Empathy.** Before you can understand someone else, you must understand yourself.

⊷ **Flexibility.** Having the willingness to change who you are when it makes sense is integral to Self-awareness.

⊷ **Humor.** Laughing at yourself is fundamental to being self-aware.

⊷ **Intelligence.** In order to understand each of the five elements of Intelligence, your Self-awareness must be finely tuned.

⊷ **Optimism.** Believing in yourself and others in a positive light helps tremendously in assessing yourself.

⊷ **Perseverance.** It's pretty tough to set goals, create a plan, and make things happen if you're not really sure about who you are and what you're capable of.

⊷ **Respect.** Self-awareness gives you the tools to influence your behavior toward others.

about his behavior, ask his permission to inform him if he exhibits the same behavior again.

If you are his manager: No doubt your employee's lack of Self-awareness extends into other aspects of his work. If this is the case, it's a good idea to explain to him that his deficiency is an important developmental need. It's true that Self-awareness is one of the most difficult Keys to learn, but it can be developed over time. There are some exercises later in this chapter that you can encourage your employee to engage in.

If you are less senior: It's always acceptable to let someone you work with know that his or her behavior is unkind or rude as long as you communicate your message diplomatically. Yes, it takes courage to do this, and often it may seem easier to suffer in silence. If the senior person is behaving badly and is oblivious to the effect his behavior is having on you, it's likely that he'd want to know. Just because someone lacks Self-awareness doesn't mean he's not a good person.

Someone gets legitimate feedback about something work related from you or a colleague and he reacts defensively or is overtly disbelieving.

If you are a peer: If you are the person who has given your coworker feedback, hopefully you've done so in a respectful manner. Is your coworker upset because he doesn't believe that your feedback is on target or simply because he doesn't receive feedback easily? Remember that when you do give feedback, always talk about how his behavior has affected business rather than about his personality.

If you are his manager: The advice for someone's peer is the same for you as his manager. The difference is that you should try to help your direct report become more in tune with himself and how he affects others. Recommend some of the activities listed later in this chapter.

If you are less senior: Again, it can be challenging to determine whether or not your manager lacks Self-awareness or is just offended by feedback. Just because someone has risen in the ranks of a company hierarchy doesn't mean he has well-developed Self-awareness. The good news is that you or your coworker had the courage to give him feedback.

Someone either doesn't have enough of or overuses one of the other Keys as a result of lacking Self-awareness.

If you are a peer: If your colleague is a poor decision-maker or isn't respectful, there are plenty of tips for dealing with her in those specific chapters. However, the fundamental issue with Self-awareness is that when someone lacks this specific Key, her ability to develop any of the other Keys will be stymied. A good first step to helping your coworker look inside herself is to keep giving her helpful feedback about how her indecisiveness or disrespectful behavior affects others. Hopefully, she will begin to make the connection between her attitudes and actions and how she connects with the outside world.

If you are her manager: If a specific incident has occurred with your low Self-awareness employee involving the other Keys, ask her to sit down and remember what she was thinking, how she felt physically and emotionally, and how these things made her respond to others. Alicia admitted to her manager that she can feel her body temperature rise considerably before she launches into an emotional tirade. Her manager suggested to Alicia that she think of a different action to take as soon as she feels her body warming up, such as excusing herself and leaving the room or drinking a big gulp of water. As difficult as it can be for someone to become more self-aware, most emotions and behaviors are habitual, and new habitual emotions and behaviors can be learned.

If you are less senior: It's important to remember that your manager is human, too. She feels pressure, stress, insecurity, and all the same things that affect you in your job. Unfortunately, there is usually an underlying reason for someone's attitude or behavior that may have nothing to do with the issue at hand. Knowing this can help you to first try to understand what your boss's intentions were when she misused one of the Keys. Understanding what this is will help you to realize why she behaved the way she did. It's still necessary for her to realize that her emotions, intentions, or behavior affected you or your colleagues counterproductively. If she isn't aware of it, there's little hope that she will change.

How accurate is your Self-awareness? Studies show that the accuracy of someone's level of Self-awareness ranges from 20 percent to 50 percent. You may be very aware of your physiology or assumptions and not as aware of your intentions or emotions.

ASSESS YOUR SELF-AWARENESS

Take the following assessment to help you decide just how well you understand yourself and your reactions, emotions, and intentions. Indicate the degree to which you agree with each statement by circling the response that best describes you.

1. I can immediately sense when my body changes physiologically.
   Almost always   Sometimes   Rarely

2. I can accurately communicate whatever I am feeling.
   Almost always   Sometimes   Rarely

3. I am able to change my moods when I want to.
   Almost always   Sometimes   Rarely

4. I am always quite aware of how my emotions and actions affect my coworkers.
   Almost always   Sometimes   Rarely

5. I can calm myself down when I am upset or angry.
   Almost always   Sometimes   Rarely

6. I rarely disagree when someone at work makes a comment about my attitude or behavior, provided it's an honest assessment.
   Almost always   Sometimes   Rarely

7. It would be easy for me to write down all my personality traits, strengths, and weaknesses.

   Almost always   Sometimes   Rarely

8. I am able to use self-talk to manage my emotions.

   Almost always   Sometimes   Rarely

9. I constantly work at accepting, expressing, and improving myself.

   Almost always   Sometimes   Rarely

10. I am quite open to and ask for constructive feedback from others.

    Almost always   Sometimes   Rarely

SCORE KEY

Write down the number of times you circled the answer "Almost always": _____.

Write down the number of times you circled the answer "Sometimes": _____.

Write down the number of times you circled the answer "Rarely": _____.

If you circled "Almost always" six or more times:

You are impressively self-aware. Your ability to monitor and change your own moods and emotions, actions, intentions, and behavior is very strong. Because of this, you are usually quite in tune with the effect you have on your colleagues. This doesn't mean that you always pay attention to your Self-awareness. It does mean that when you put your heart into changing, you are able to do so effectively.

If you circled "Sometimes" six or more times:

Much of the time you are aware of how you should respond, behave, and communicate with people at work. You may be closely in tune with some aspects of yourself such as your moods or emotions but not so much with other aspects such as your physical appearance and your behavior. You have the capacity to increase your Self-awareness even more so.

If you circled "Rarely" four or more times:

Your Self-awareness is dangerously low. This means you are not too cognizant of how you come across to others or how to manage your moods, behavior, and presence. Your low level of Self-awareness makes it challenging to develop any of the other Keys easily or effectively. If your score fell into this category, keep reading to choose some exercises that will help you to increase your Self-awareness.

TIPS AND TECHNIQUES FOR IMPROVING YOUR SELF-AWARENESS

Here are some exercises that will help you to become more self-aware.

Be Curious About Yourself

Most people tend to become either more or less curious with age. When they reach middle age, some people can become set in their ways and stop trying to understand how they come across to others. In all fairness, young people can be just as guilty of not taking risks or not trying new things. Regardless of age, curiosity is a motivational state, which can emerge, change focus, or end abruptly, depending on the circumstances. Much of the time, people may not try to learn more about themselves, and how others view them, until circumstances force them to do so. Stephen is a perfect example of this. Recently, Stephen lost the job he had held for eighteen years. The day he was fired, his boss inadvertently revealed that several of Stephen's colleagues found him to be rigid and unapproachable. Stephen's wife has given him this feedback for years, but when he heard his boss say it on the day he lost his job, his boss's comment stuck with him. When he met with his outplacement counselor, Stephen confided in her that he was embarrassed to have been viewed as inflexible by his peers. There were probably many signs that people at Stephen's company felt this way about him but, sadly, he wasn't motivated to pay attention to this feedback until it was too late to salvage the situation.

Other people become more curious and introspective as they age. They do a kind of life review assessment and become motivated to make changes in those attitudes and behaviors that may not have worked well for them in the past. The Key Curiosity is naturally a huge driver in this process. Reading about each of the Eleven Keys will help you to discover which may be your areas of strength and which may be areas you need to work on. Make a list of five people you trust and whose opinions you respect. Write down each person's name and relationship to you here:

1. _____
2. _____
3. _____
4. _____
5. _____

Next, think of several specific questions you can ask each person on your list to answer *honestly* to help you learn more about yourself. Here are some examples: What is one thing I can do more of to enhance our relationship?

_____
_____
_____

Can you name three qualities or traits I have that you wouldn't change?

_____
_____
_____

If you could change one thing about me, what would it be and why?

_____
_____
_____

Do I have a strength that you think I could use in a different, more effective way?

_____
_____
_____

If you could give me one piece of advice to help me succeed at work, what would it be?

_____
_____
_____

Getting candid answers to these or similar questions is a great way to help you learn more about yourself and become more thoughtful about how you react and behave at work.

Write Your Own Eulogy

This exercise is typically used with someone who is going through a transition of some kind and needs to become more knowledgeable about himself in order to make the transition successful. Find a quiet place, sit down, and write two paragraphs that someone who knows you would read at your funeral or memorial service. Be as candid as possible and focus on the truth.

_____

_____

_____

_____

Walk or Drive to Get Lost

Go for a walk and keep walking until you don't know where you are (be sure to bring your cell phone) or go for a drive with the same goal. Then try to find your way back. Be very conscious of your emotions, feelings, and behavior (anger, frustration, boredom). Forcing yourself into an uncomfortable or meaningless activity such as this will cause you to pay attention to yourself in a different way. Write below how you felt. Did your feelings surprise you? If so,why?

_____

_____

_____

_____

360-Degree Feedback

If you are fortunate enough to work for a company that offers profiling-assessment tools, ask your manager if you can participate in a 360-degree feedback process. This involves selecting six to ten coworkers with whom you have different relationships (peer, boss, client, etc.) and asking them to anonymously answer a series of questions about you and your behavior at work. At the same time, you'll answer all the same questions about yourself. This is always an eye-opener for even the most self-aware! The idea is to focus on the areas that your colleagues have indicated could be improved. If you don't work for a company that offers this development perk, create a list of your own questions and ask your coworkers to answer them.

Ask Yourself Questions

So many people walk through life without understanding who they are and what's really important to them. What is strange about this is that you are the greatest expert about yourself—not your spouse, minister, parents, siblings, friends, or coworkers. Answering questions about yourself can make you more self-aware. The following questions are broken down by categories: social, emotional, career, and personal. Be as specific as you can in your answers and avoid judging yourself or worrying about what the "right" answer should be. Be very honest, and if you're not sure of an answer, force yourself to try to respond anyway.

Social
What type of people do I like to spend time with?

_____

_____

_____

Why do I like to spend time with these people?

_____

_____

_____

Do I have many friends or acquaintances of the type I just described?

_____

_____

_____

If not, why not?

_____
_____
_____

What are two or three things I enjoy doing with other people?

_____
_____
_____

How often do I do these things?

_____
_____
_____

Do I have friends whom I don't enjoy? If so, why?

_____
_____
_____

How would I like my friends and people in my social circle to view me?

_____
_____
_____

Do they view me this way now?

_____
_____
_____

Emotional

What do I fear most happening in my life right now?

_____
_____
_____

What would it mean if it happened?

_____

_____

_____

What makes me feel angry or frustrated?

_____

_____

_____

What makes me happy?

_____

_____

_____

Do I have control over my emotions?

_____

_____

_____

What emotions do I want to feel most of the time?

_____

_____

_____

Career

What types of things did I enjoy doing as a child?

_____

_____

_____

Am I doing work today that shares some of the same qualities? If so, what are they? If not, why not?

_____

_____

_____

What do I like about my work?

_____

_____

_____

What don't I like about my work?

_____

_____

_____

What is my definition of success?

_____

_____

_____

Personal

What accomplishments am I most proud of?

_____

_____

_____

What are the three or four most significant events in my life so far?

_____

_____

_____

What period in my life have I liked the most? Why?

_____

_____

_____

_____

What period in my life have I liked the least? Why?

_____

_____

_____

_____

What do I desire the most right now?

_____

_____

_____

_____

What would I keep the same forever?

_____

_____

_____

_____

The Eleven Keys

Which of the Eleven Keys do I want to improve (increase or downplay)? Why?

_____

_____

_____

_____

Which of the Eleven Keys do I possess a balance of?

_____

_____

_____

CREATE AN ACTION PLAN

Ashley keeps getting feedback from her boss and coworkers about her behavior, and it never seems to jibe with the way she sees herself. Finally, in her most recent performance appraisal, her boss told Ashley that she really needs to become more self-aware. One of the specific areas he mentioned is her nonverbal communication. She has decided to write an action plan. Here it is:

MY GOAL: I would like to dramatically increase my Self-awareness about how my nonverbal communication affects other people.

MY SHORT-TERM OBJECTIVE/ACTIVITY IS:
Role-play a meeting with one of my friends and ask my husband to videotape it so I can see how I come across nonverbally.

MY MEDIUM-TERM OBJECTIVE/ACTIVITY IS:
Create a development plan with the help of my friend Nancy who works as an executive coach. She is familiar with lots of resources that will help me.

MY LONG-TERM OBJECTIVE/ACTIVITY IS:
Implement the development plan over a six-month period of time, periodically asking my boss for feedback on my improvement.

Now, fill out your own action plan, keeping it simple, just like Ashley did.

Our goal:

_____

_____

My short-term objectives/activities are:

_____

_____

_____

By when: _____

My medium-term objectives/activities are:

_____

_____

_____

By when: _____

My long-term objectives/activities are:

_____

_____

_____

By when: _____

University of New Hampshire professor John Mayer has found that people who are very self-aware are more sophisticated emotionally, are in better psychological health than most, and tend to have a positive outlook on life. Someone who is truly self-aware sees the need to change interpersonal and managerial behavior quickly, watches others for their reactions to his or her attempts to influence and perform, seeks feedback, and is responsive to needed changes in personal demands.

Self-awareness is often taken for granted until it becomes glaringly obvious that someone is missing it. In Zen Buddhism, ignorance of one's own self is viewed as the source of much human suffering.

Afterword

Recently, I coached Phyllis, a managing editor of a major business magazine, whose employer hired me to help her strengthen her management skills, such as coaching and motivating employees, giving feedback, and delegating work. After our first meeting, I quickly realized that giving Phyllis a tutorial about the steps to learning how to do these things would not be an effective approach because she already believed that she was a pretty good manager despite the overwhelming feedback from her direct reports that she was not.

Instead, I asked Phyllis to assess her effectiveness with each of the Eleven Keys on a scale of 1 to 5. I also asked her boss to tell me which of the Keys were her strengths and which needed development, and I asked Phyllis to choose a few of her direct reports to do the same. Once we had organized the feedback, it was obvious that Phyllis had trouble making decisions (Key #3: Decisiveness), didn't try to understand her staff's situations and feelings (Key #4: Empathy), wasn't very willing to try different approaches with the magazine or to listen to creative story ideas that her staff would pitch to her (Key #5: Flexibility), ran roughshod over her staff in meetings (Key #10: Respect), and didn't realize that her behavior affected her staff and colleagues detrimentally (Key #11: Self-awareness).

Once Phyllis was able to absorb the feedback she had received about herself in the context of the specific Keys, we discussed how Phyllis's deficiency in five of the Eleven Keys negatively affected her ability to successfully manage her people. We then laid out a plan for Phyllis to develop the Keys in the context of each specific management skill, such as giving feedback and delegating tasks. For example, in the past, Phyllis would give one of her direct reports negative feedback in the hallway in front of anyone standing there without scripting it first or thinking about what she wanted that person to do differently. When we discussed the need for Phyllis to empathize with her employee, be self-aware of how she was coming across to the person, and behave in a professional and sensitive manner, she realized why her employee had not responded favorably in the past.

Phyllis's Decisiveness was rated low by everyone who responded to the survey because she had a habit of delaying her decisions, finally making one and then changing her mind the next day. This pattern of behavior adversely affected everyone else's work because they would then have to change their position based upon whatever Phyllis decided. Once Phyllis realized how dysfunctional her decision-making was, we identified a process that Phyllis would use for each decision she was faced with.

After six months of working together and having Phyllis practice new techniques for strengthening the five Keys, we surveyed her direct reports, boss, and several colleagues. The results were wonderfully positive and dramatically different from our interviews with Phyllis's coworkers when we began working together.

The Eleven Keys are powerful tools to use in developing leadership skills, improving relationships, reaching mutual goals, and achieving anything, no matter who you're working for or with. If you have read this book and know which of the Eleven Keys you can develop more fully or use to work more happily and effectively with your colleagues, it's time to get started. There is no doubt in my mind that by using these Keys and doing the required exercises to fine-tune the Keys within your own life, you will build lasting, productive relationships, your satisfaction will increase, your stress will diminish, and your overall success at work will skyrocket!

Resources

THE ELEVEN KEYS
Books

Emotional Intelligence Quickbook, by Travis Bradberry and Jean Greaves. Talent Smart, 2003.

Pulling Your Own Strings, by Dr. Wayne W. Dyer. Avon Books, 1978.

The Emotional Intelligence Activity Book: 50 Activities for Promoting EQ at Work, by Adele B. Lynn. American Management Association, 2001.

Emotional Intelligence at Work, by Hendrie Weisinger. Jossey-Bass, 1998.

Leadership Through People Skills, by Robert E. Lefton and Victor R. Buzzotta, McGraw Hill, 2004.

DIFFICULT PEOPLE
Books

Problem People at Work, by Marilyn Wheeler. St. Martin's Griffin, 1995.

Who's That Sitting at My Desk? by Jan Yager. Hannacroix Creek Books, 2004.

A Survival Guide for Working with Humans: Dealing with Whiners, Back-Stabbers, Know-It-Alls, and Other Difficult People, by Gini Graham Scott. Amacom, 2004.

KEY #1: CONFIDENCE
Books

Self-Esteem at Work: How Confident People Make Powerful Companies, by Nathaniel Brandon. Jossey-Bass, 1998.

Complete Confidence: A Handbook, by Sheenah Hankin. Regan Books, 2004.

How to Have Confidence and Power in Dealing with People, by Les Giblin. Prentice Hall Art, 1985.

Confidence: How Winning Streaks and Losing Streaks Begin and End, by Rosabeth Moss Kanter. Crown Business, 2004.

The Ultimate Secrets of Total Self-Confidence, by Robert Anthony. Berkley Publishing Group, 1994.

The Confidence Course: Seven Steps to Self-Fulfillment, by Walter Anderson. Perennial, 1998.

Web Sites

www.confidenceworld.com

www.hamr.com/self-confidence/self-confidence.php

www.ivillage.co.uk/workcareer/confidence

www.mindtools.com/selfconf.html

www.thecompanypsychologist.com

Movies to Watch

Patton (1970)

Ray (2004)

Rocky (1976)

KEY #2: CURIOSITY
Web Sites

teacher.scholastic.com/professional/bruceperry/curiosity.htm

www.beswick.info/psychres/curiosityintro.htm

www.acsu.buffalo.edu/~kashdan/ampsy.curiosity.html

Movies to Watch

Dances with Wolves (1990)

The Sixth Sense (1999)

Rear Window (1954)

12 Angry Men (1957)

KEY #3: DECISIVENESS
Books

Sources of Power: How People Make Decisions, by Gary Klein. MIT Press, reprint edition, 1999.

Winning Decisions: Getting It Right the First Time, by J. Edward Russo. Currency, 2001.

Why Decisions Fail, by Paul C. Nutt. Berrett-Koehler, 2002.

Smart Choices: A Practical Guide to Making Better Life Decisions, by John S. Hammond. Broadway Books, 2002.

Web Sites

www.nova.edu/~rawll/edl530/week2.html

admfin.wcu.edu/hr/dod/Decisiveness.htm

Movies to Watch

Norma Rae (1979)

Citizen Kane (1941)

KEY #4: EMPATHY
Books

How to Win Friends and Influence People, by Dale Carnegie. Pocket Books, reissue edition, 1990.

Toxic Emotions at Work, by Peter Frost. Harvard Business School Press, 2003.

How to Connect in Business, by Nicholas Booth. Workman Publishing, 2002.

Everyday Mind Reading: Understanding What Other People Think and Feel, by William Ickes and Elliot Aronson. Prometheus Books, 2003.

Web Sites

www.advancingwomen.com/workplace/empathy.html

www.advancedcommunication.com.au/articles/article003.html/

Movies to Watch

On Golden Pond (1981)

The Miracle Worker (1962)

Longtime Companion (1990)

Gandhi (1982)

KEY #5: FLEXIBILITY
Books
Flexible Leadership: Creating Value by Balancing Multiple Challenges and Choices, by Richard Lepsinger and Gary Yukl. Pfeiffer, 2004.

Web Sites
cjonline.com/stories/022003/opi_flexibility.shtml

www.charactercouncil.org

Movies to Watch
Tootsie (1982)

Guess Who's Coming to Dinner (1967)

Under the Tuscan Sun (2003)

Overboard (1987)

KEY #6: HUMOR
Books
Becoming a Humor Being: The Power to Choose a Better Way, by Steve Rizzo. Full Circle Publishing Company, 2000.

Humor at Work: The Guaranteed, Bottom-Line, Low-Cost, High-Efficiency Guide to Success Through Humor, by Esther Blumenfeld and Lynne Alpern. Peachtree, 1993.

Serious Laughter: Live a Happier, Healthier, More Productive Life, by Yvonne Francine Conte. Amsterdam-Berwick, 1998.

Movies to Watch
My Big Fat Greek Wedding (2002)

Something's Gotta Give (2003)

Forrest Gump (1994)

KEY #7: INTELLIGENCE
Books
Thinkertoys: A Handbook of Business Creativity for the '90s, by Michael Michalko. Ten Speed Press, 1991.

The Personal Efficiency Program: How to Get Organized to Do More Work in Less Time, by Kerry Gleason. John Wiley & Sons, 2003.

Six Thinking Hats, by Edward De Bono. Little, Brown and Company, 1999.

Sparks of Genius: The 13 Thinking Tools of the World's Most Creative People, by Robert and Michele Root-Bernstein. Houghton Mifflin Co., 1999.

Time Tactics of Very Successful People, by Eugene Griessman. McGraw-Hill, 1994.

Order from Chaos, by Liz Davenport. Three Rivers Press, 2001.

Get Them to See It Your Way, Right Away, by Ruth Sherman. McGraw-Hill, 2004.

Getting Things Done: The Art of Stress-Free Productivity, by David Allen. Penguin Books, 2003.

Ready for Anything: 52 Productivity Principles for Work and Life, by David Allen. Viking Books, 2003.

Movies to Watch
Sneakers (1992)

A Beautiful Mind (2001)

KEY #8: OPTIMISM
Books
Half Empty, Half Full: Understanding the Psychological Roots of Optimism, by Susan C. Vaughan. Harvest Books, 2001.

The Power of Positive Thinking in Business, by Scott W. Ventrella. Simon & Schuster, 2001.

Learned Optimism: How to Change Your Mind and Your Life, by Martin Seligman. Free Press, reissue edition, 1998.

Life of Pi, by Yann Martel. Harvest Books, 2003.

Adversity Quotient: Turning Obstacles into Opportunities, by Paul Stolz. Wiley, 1999.

Movies to Watch
The Color Purple (1985)

The Shawshank Redemption (1994)

KEY #9: PERSEVERANCE
Books
Unstoppable: 45 Powerful Stories of Perseverance and Triumph from People Just Like You, by Cynthia Kersey. Sourcebooks, 1998.

The Power of Focus, by Jack Canfield, Mark Victor Hansen, and Les Hewitt. Health Communications, 2000.

Cheap Psychological Tricks: What to Do When Hard Work, Honesty, and Perseverance Fail, by Perry W. Buffington, and Mitzi Cartee. Peachtree, 1996.

When Smart People Fail: Rebuilding Yourself for Success, by Carole Hyatt and Linda Gottlieb. Penguin Books, 1993.

Perseverance, by B. Schrader. Northern Lights Publishing, 2002.

Movies to Watch

The Fugitive (1993)

Cast Away (2000)

Gone with the Wind (1939)

Rudy (1993)

Cold Mountain (2003)

KEY #10: RESPECT
Books

Respect: An Exploration, by Sara Lawrence-Lightfoot. Perseus, 2000.

Dear Parent: Caring for Infants with Respect, by Magda Gerber and Joan Weaver. SCB Distributors, 2003.

Movies to Watch

Schindler's List (1993)

Ordinary People (1980)

Driving Miss Daisy (1989)

KEY #11: SELF-AWARENESS
Books

Journey to Self-Awareness: A Spiritual Notebook for Everyday Life, by Noreen Monroe Guzie and Tad Guzie. Paulist Press, 1994.

Emotional Intelligence: Why It Can Matter More Than IQ, by Daniel Goleman. Bantam Books, 1995.

Movies to Watch

Million Dollar Baby (2004)

Legally Blonde (2001)

Index

FOR THE BEST IN PAPERBACKS, LOOK FOR THE 🐧

In every corner of the world, on every subject under the sun, Penguin represents quality and variety—the very best in publishing today.

For complete information about books available from Penguin—including Penguin Classics, Penguin Compass, and Puffins—and how to order them, write to us at the appropriate address below. Please note that for copyright reasons the selection of books varies from country to country.

In the United States: Please write to *Penguin Group (USA), P.O. Box 12289 Dept. B, Newark, New Jersey 07101-5289* or call 1-800-788-6262.

In the United Kingdom: Please write to *Dept. EP, Penguin Books Ltd, Bath Road, Harmondsworth, West Drayton, Middlesex UB7 0DA.*

In Canada: Please write to *Penguin Books Canada Ltd, 90 Eglinton Avenue East, Suite 700, Toronto, Ontario M4P 2Y3.*

In Australia: Please write to *Penguin Books Australia Ltd, P.O. Box 257, Ringwood, Victoria 3134.*

In New Zealand: Please write to *Penguin Books (NZ) Ltd, Private Bag 102902, North Shore Mail Centre, Auckland 10.*

In India: Please write to *Penguin Books India Pvt Ltd, 11 Panchsheel Shopping Centre, Panchsheel Park, New Delhi 110 017.*

In the Netherlands: Please write to *Penguin Books Netherlands bv, Postbus 3507, NL-1001 AH Amsterdam.*

In Germany: Please write to *Penguin Books Deutschland GmbH, Metzlerstrasse 26, 60594 Frankfurt am Main.*

In Spain: Please write to *Penguin Books S. A., Bravo Murillo 19, 1° B, 28015 Madrid.*

In Italy: Please write to *Penguin Italia s.r.l., Via Benedetto Croce 2, 20094 Corsico, Milano.*

In France: Please write to *Penguin France, Le Carré Wilson, 62 rue Benjamin Baillaud, 31500 Toulouse.*

In Japan: Please write to *Penguin Books Japan Ltd, Kaneko Building, 2-3-25 Koraku, Bunkyo-Ku, Tokyo 112.*

In South Africa: Please write to *Penguin Books South Africa (Pty) Ltd, Private Bag X14, Parkview, 2122 Johannesburg.*